SELECTIONS FROM O BROTHER, WHERE ART THOU?

2 **THE BIG ROCK CANDY MOUNTAIN**
Harry McClintock

6 **YOU ARE MY SUNSHINE**
Norman Blake

10 **DOWN TO THE RIVER TO PRAY**
Alison Krauss

9 **I AM A MAN OF CONSTANT SORROW**
Norman Blake

12 **KEEP ON THE SUNNY SIDE**
The Whites

16 **I'LL FLY AWAY**
Alison Krauss and Gillian Welch

24 **DIDN'T LEAVE NOBODY BUT THE BABY**
Emmylou Harris, Alison Krauss and Gillian Welch

21 **IN THE HIGHWAYS (I'LL BE SOMEWHERE WORKING FOR MY LORD)**
Sarah, Hannah and Leah Peasall

26 **I AM WEARY (LET ME REST)**
The Cox Family

29 **IN THE JAILHOUSE NOW**
The Soggy Bottom Boys

33 **I AM A MAN OF CONSTANT SORROW**
The Soggy Bottom Boys

37 **ANGEL BAND**
The Stanley Brothers

40 **BANJO NOTATION LEGEND**

T0055439

Artwork and photos courtesy of Touchstone Pictures

Arranged by Jim Schustedt

ISBN 978-0-634-04902-6

HAL•LEONARD® CORPORATION
7777 W. BLUEMOUND RD. P.O. BOX 13819 MILWAUKEE, WI 53213

For all works contained herein:
Unauthorized copying, arranging, adapting, recording or public performance is an infringement of copyright.
Infringers are liable under the law.

Visit Hal Leonard Online at
www.halleonard.com

The Big Rock Candy Mountain

Words, Music and Arrangement by Harry K. McClintock

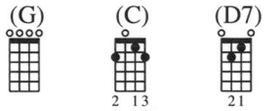

G tuning:
(5th-1st) G–D–G–B–D
Capo V
Key of C

Intro
Moderately

C
* (G)

1. One

Verse
C
(G)

eve - ning as the sun went down and the jun - gle fire was burn - ing, down the

track came a ho - bo hik - in' and he said, "Boys, I'm not

* Symbols in parentheses represent chord names respective to capoed banjo.
Symbols above reflect actual sounding chords. Capoed fret is "0" in tab.

Copyright © 1955 by The Estate of Harry McClintock
Copyright Renewed
All Rights Reserved Used by Permission

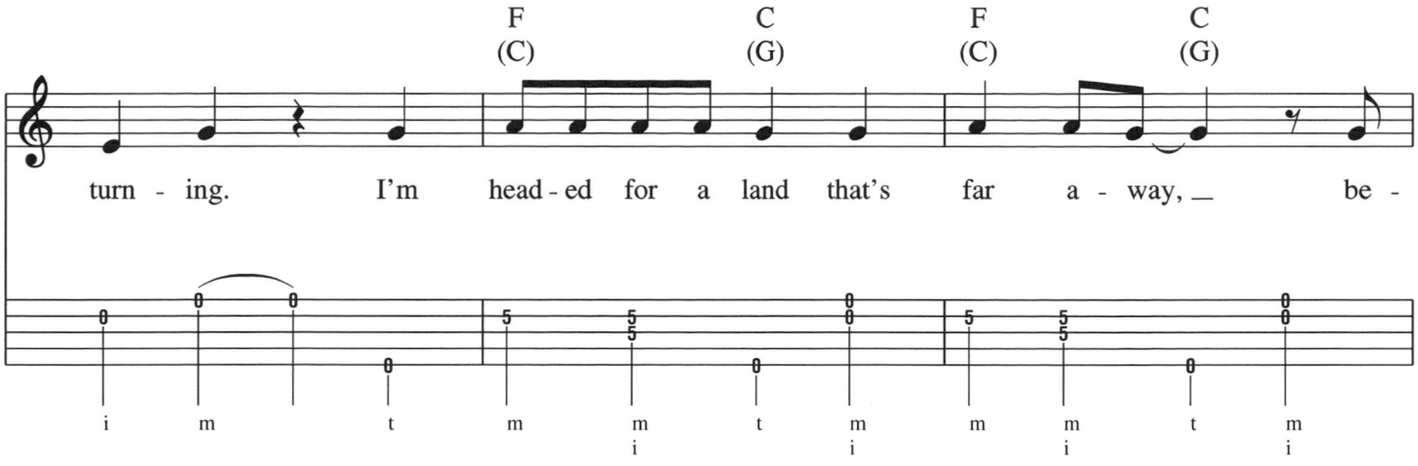
F (C) C (G) F (C) C (G)
turn - ing. I'm head - ed for a land that's far a - way, be -

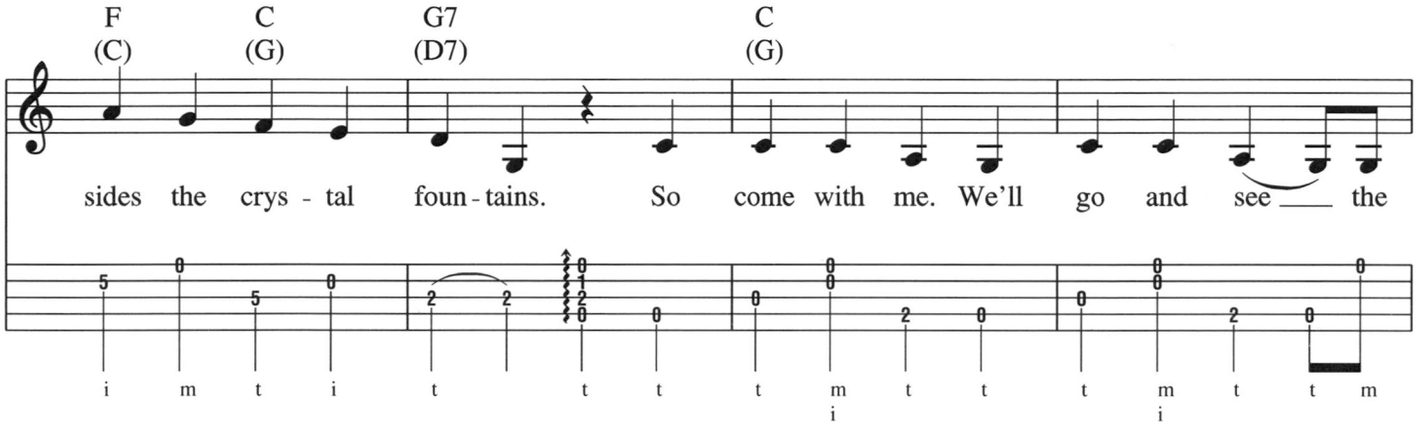
F (C) C (G) G7 (D7) C (G)
sides the crys - tal foun - tains. So come with me. We'll go and see the

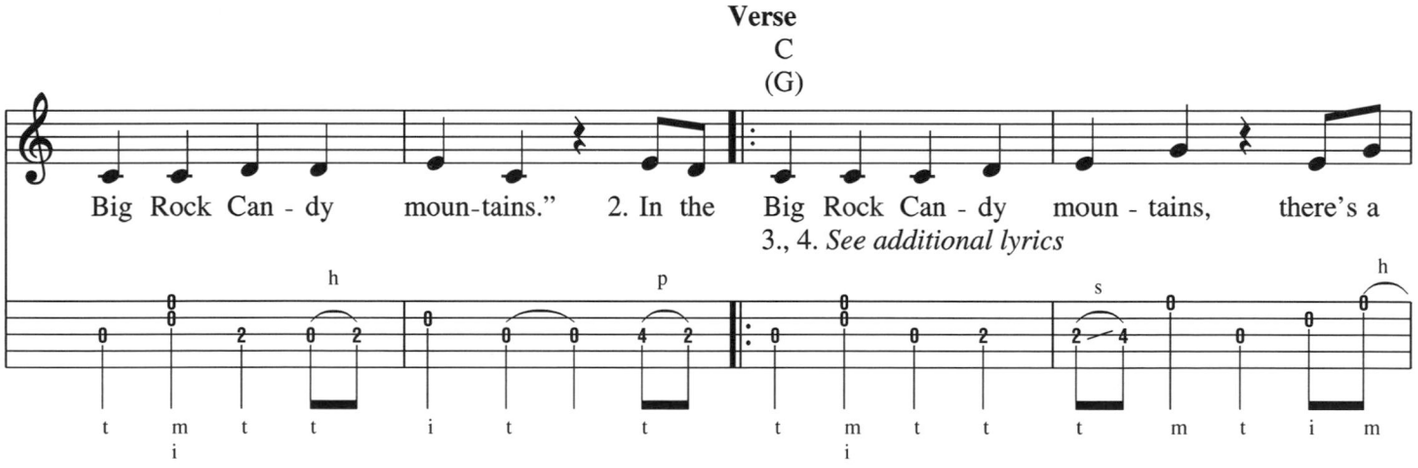
Verse
C (G)
Big Rock Can - dy moun - tains." 2. In the Big Rock Can - dy moun - tains, there's a
3., 4. See additional lyrics

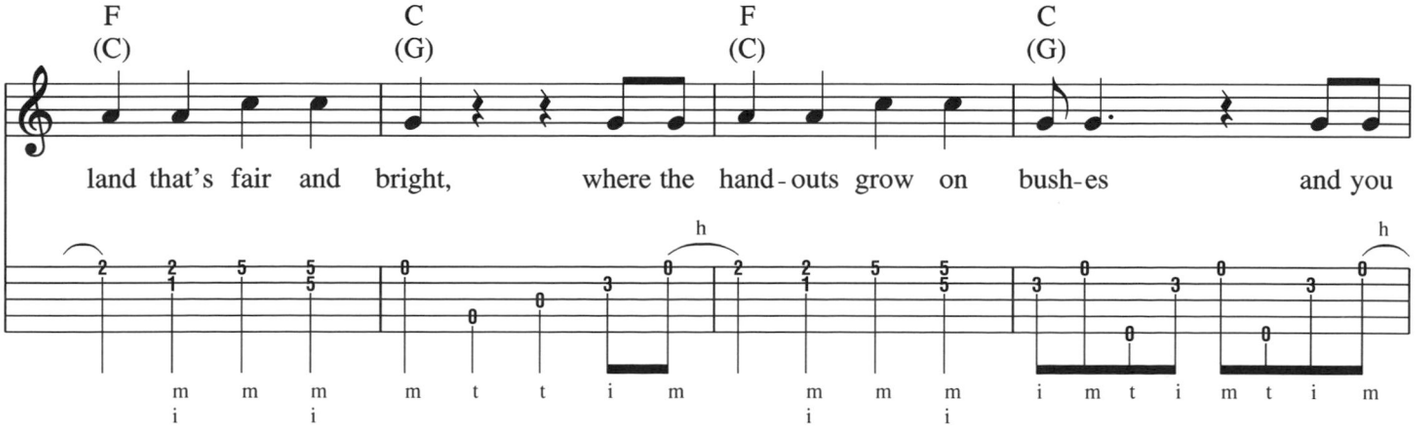
F (C) C (G) F (C) C (G)
land that's fair and bright, where the hand - outs grow on bush - es and you

G7 (D7)
C (G)
sleep out ev - 'ry night. Where the box - cars all are emp - ty and the
F (C)
C (G)
F (C)
C (G)
F (C)
C (G)
sun shines ev - 'ry day ___ on the birds and the bees and the cig - a - rette trees, the
F (C)
C (G)
F (C)
C (G)
G7 (D7)
lem - on - ade springs where the blue - bird sings in the Big Rock Can - dy
1., 2., 3.
C (G)
moun - tains.
3. In the moun - tains. Whistled:
4.
C (G)
Outro
C (G)

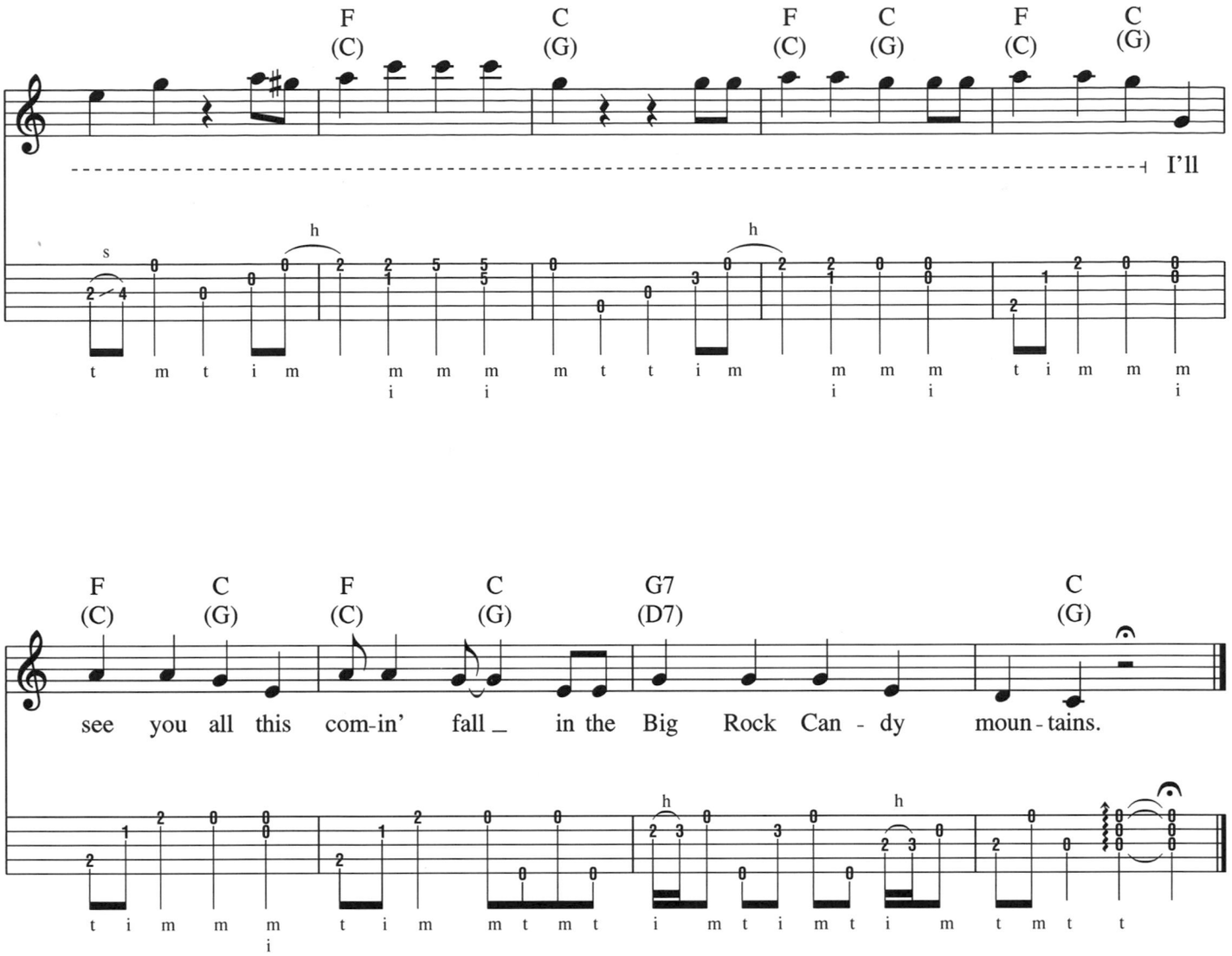

Additional Lyrics

3. In the Big Rock Candy mountains, all the cops have wooden legs
   And the bulldogs all have rubber teeth and the hens lay soft boiled eggs.
   The farmers' trees are full of fruit and the barns are full of hay.
   Oh, I'm bound to go where there ain't no snow,
   Where the rain don't fall, the wind don't blow
   In the Big Rock Candy mountains.

4. In the Big Rock Candy mountains, you never change your socks
   And the little streams of alcohol come a trickling down the rocks.
   The brakeman have to tip their hats and the railroad bulls are blind.
   There's a lake of stew and of whiskey too.
   You can paddle all around 'em in a big canoe
   In the Big Rock Candy mountains.

5. In the Big Rock Candy mountains, the jails are made of tin
   And you can walk right out again as soon as you are in.
   There ain't no short handled shovels, no axes, saws or picks.
   I'm a goin' to stay where you sleep all day,
   Where they hung the jerk that invented work,
   In the Big Rock Candy mountains.

You Are My Sunshine

Words and Music by Jimmie Davis and Charles Mitchell

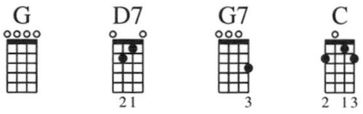

G tuning, down 1/2 step:
(5th-1st) G♭–D♭–G♭–B♭–D♭

Key of G

Intro
Moderately

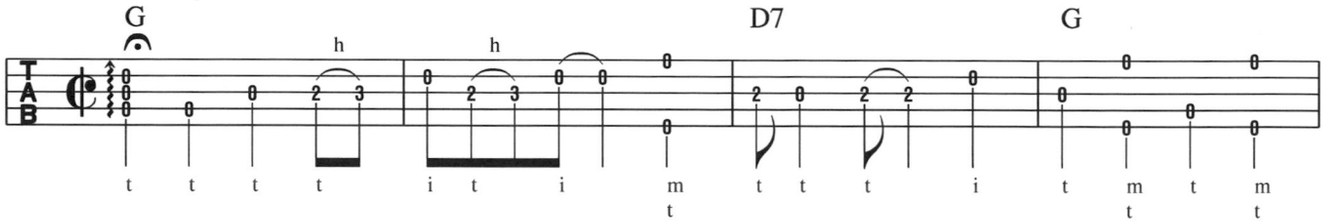

Verse

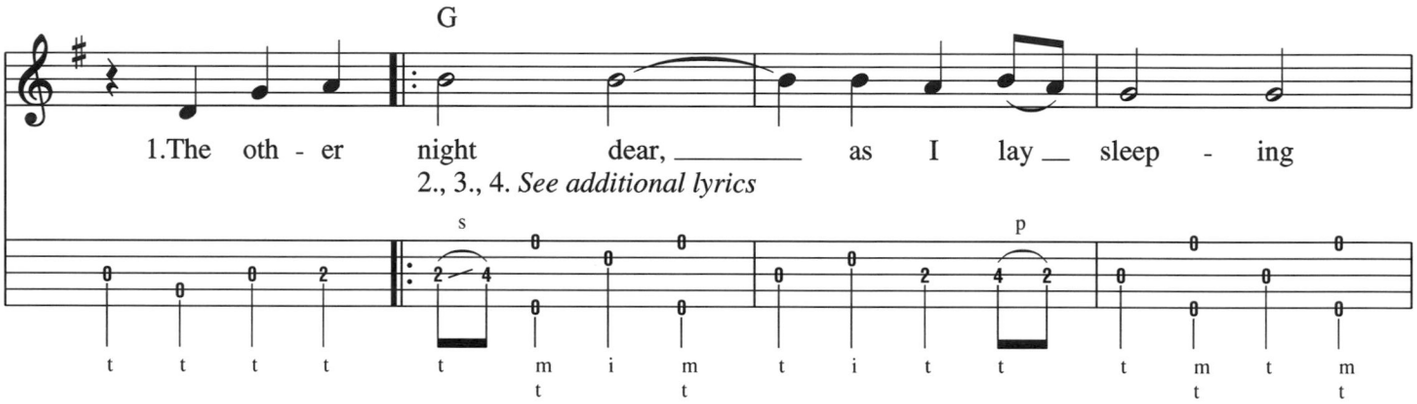

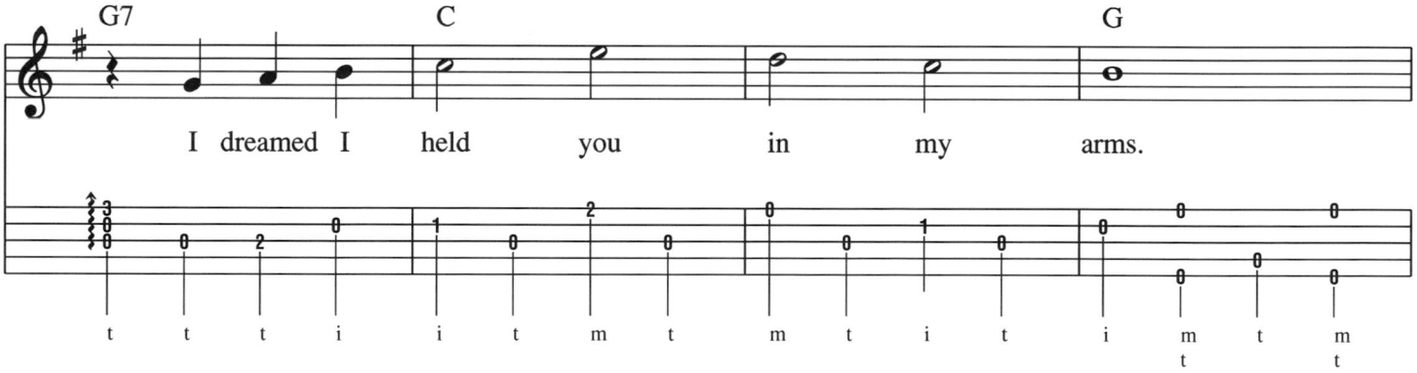

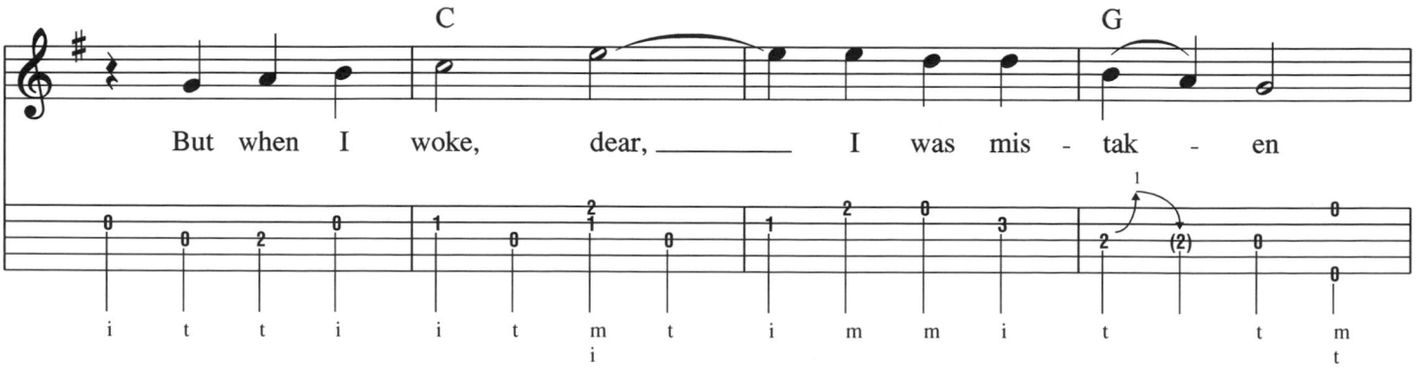

Copyright © 1930 by Peer International Corporation
Copyright Renewed
International Copyright Secured All Rights Reserved

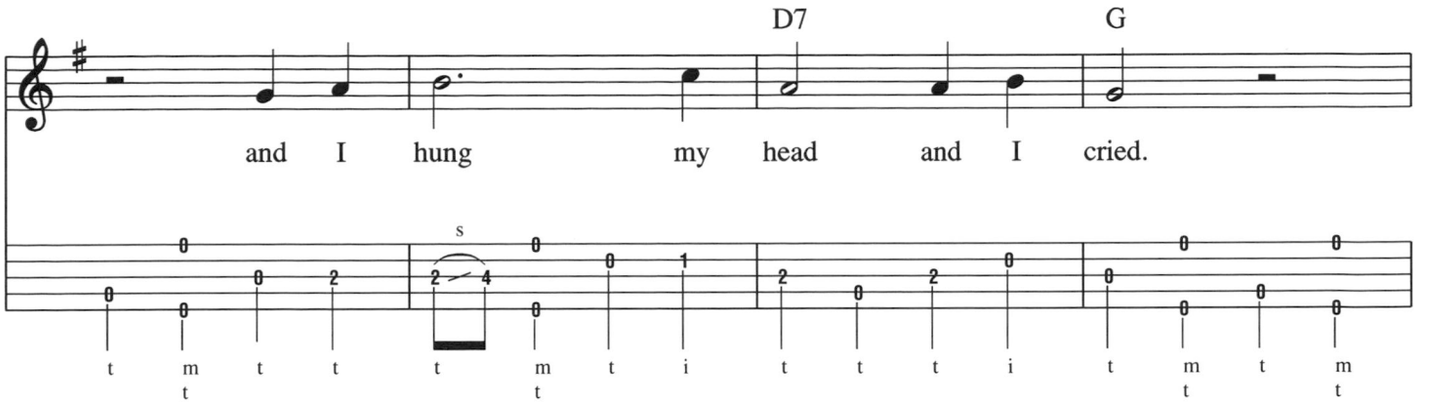
D7
G
and I hung my head and I cried.

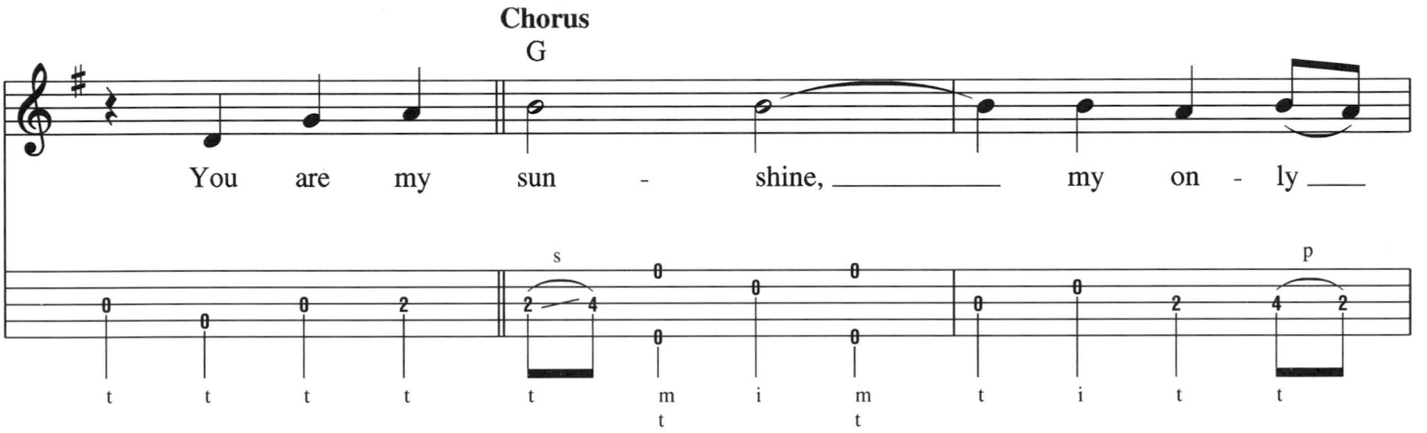
Chorus
G
You are my sun - shine, my on - ly

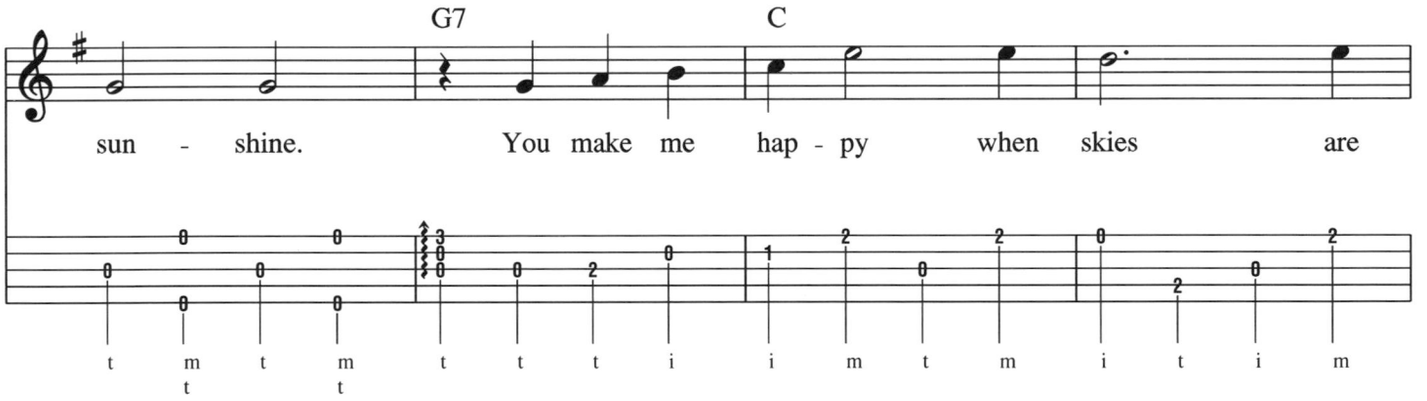
G7
C
sun - shine. You make me hap - py when skies are

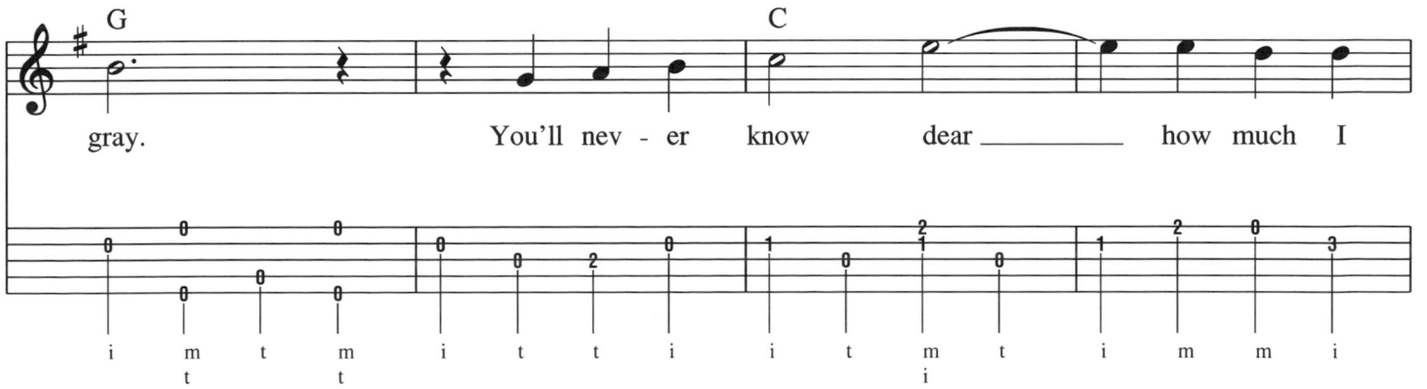
G
C
gray. You'll nev - er know dear how much I

Additional Lyrics

2. I'll always love you and make you happy
   If you will only say the same.
   But if you leave me and love another,
   You'll regret it all some day.

3. You told me once, dear, you really loved me
   And no one could come between.
   But now you've left me to love another.
   You have shattered all of my dreams.

4. In all my dreams, dear, you seem to leave me.
   When I awake my poor heart pains.
   So won't you come back and make me happy.
   I'll forgive, dear, I'll take the blame.

I Am a Man of Constant Sorrow

Words and Music by Carter Stanley

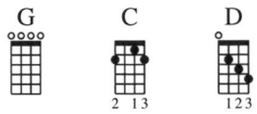

G tuning:
(5th-1st) G–D–G–B–D
Key of G

Moderately

G

C

1. - 13.

D

G

14.

D

rit.

G

Copyright © 1953 by Peer International Corporation
Copyright Renewed
International Copyright Secured All Rights Reserved

Down to the River to Pray

Traditional

* 6th time, *ritard*

Copyright © 2002 by HAL LEONARD CORPORATION
International Copyright Secured All Rights Reserved

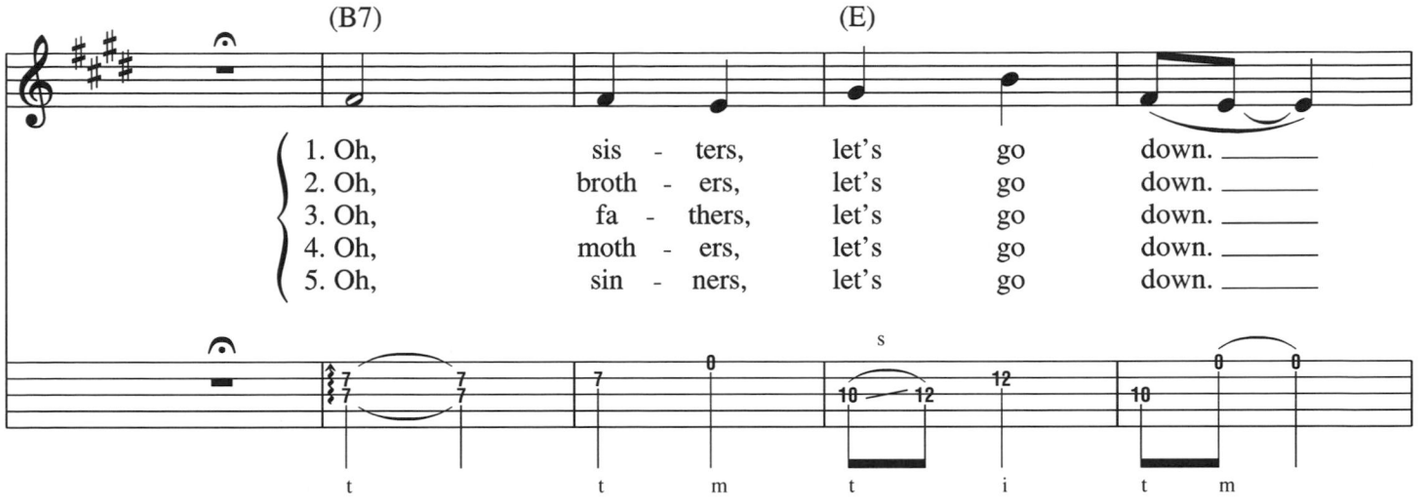

*5th time, **D.C. al Fine*

** Repeat back to the beginning of the song and play until the directive ***Fine.***

Keep on the Sunny Side

Words and Music by A.P. Carter

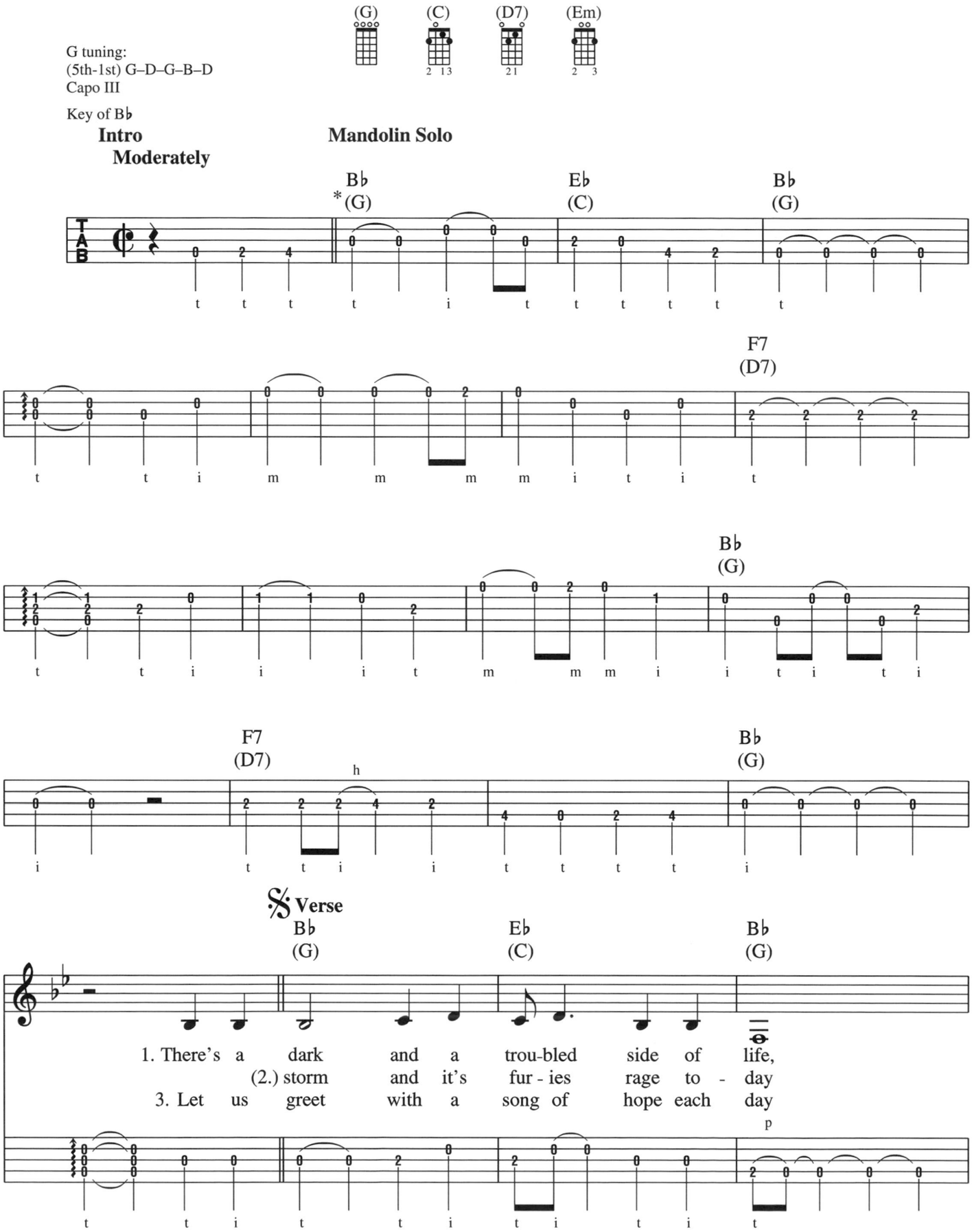

* Symbols in parentheses represent chord names respective to capoed banjo.
Symbols above reflect actual sounding chords. Capoed fret is "0" in tab.

Copyright © 1928 by Peer International Corporation
Copyright Renewed
International Copyright Secured All Rights Reserved

F7
(D7)
but there's a bright and a sun-ny side too.
crush-ing hope that we cher-ish so dear.
though the mo-ment be cloud-y or fair.
B♭
(G)
Though you meet with the dark-ness and strife,
The cloud and storm will in time pass a-way
And let us trust in our Sav-ior al-ways.
F7
(D7)
B♭
(G)
the sun-ny side you al-so may view.
and the sun a-gain will shine bright and clear.
He'll keep us, ev-'ry-one, in His care.
Chorus
B♭
(G)
E♭
(C)
Keep on the sun-ny side, al-ways on the

**** 3rd time, D.S.S. al Coda 2***

Dobro Solo

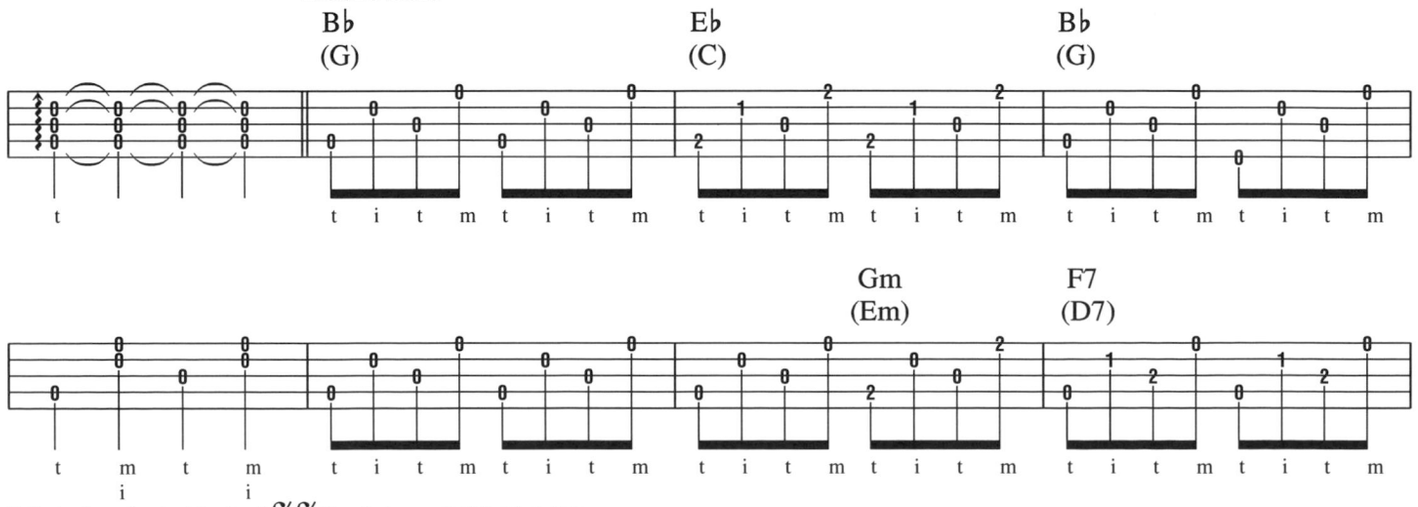

* Go back to the double sign " 𝄋𝄋 " and play until ***"To Coda 2,"*** then skip ahead to the section labeled **"Coda 2."**

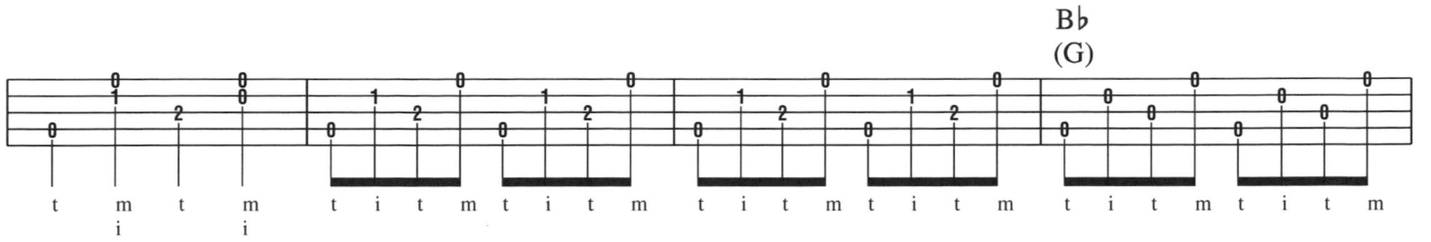

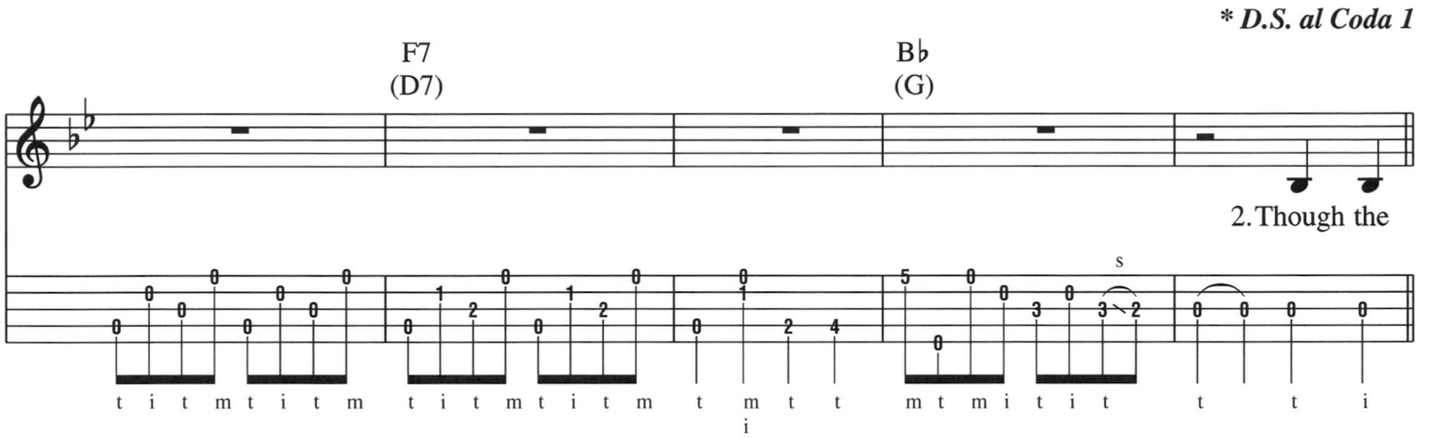

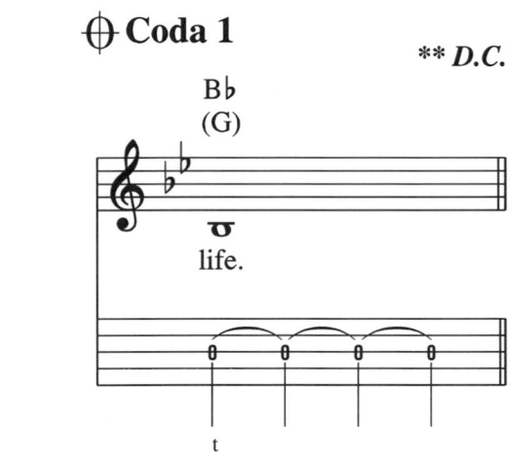

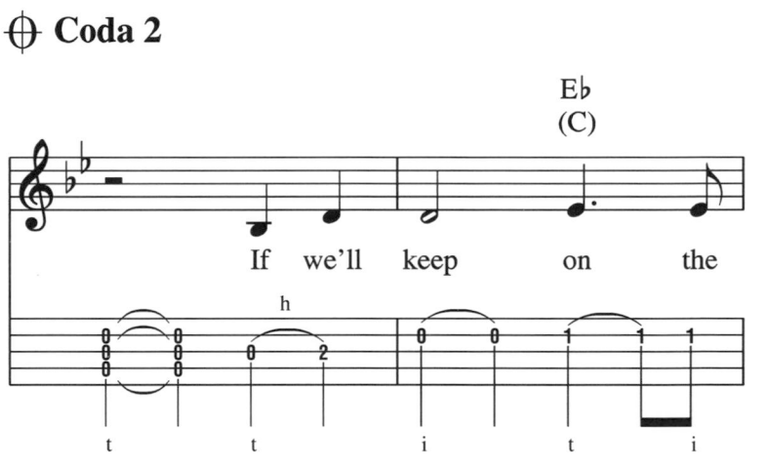

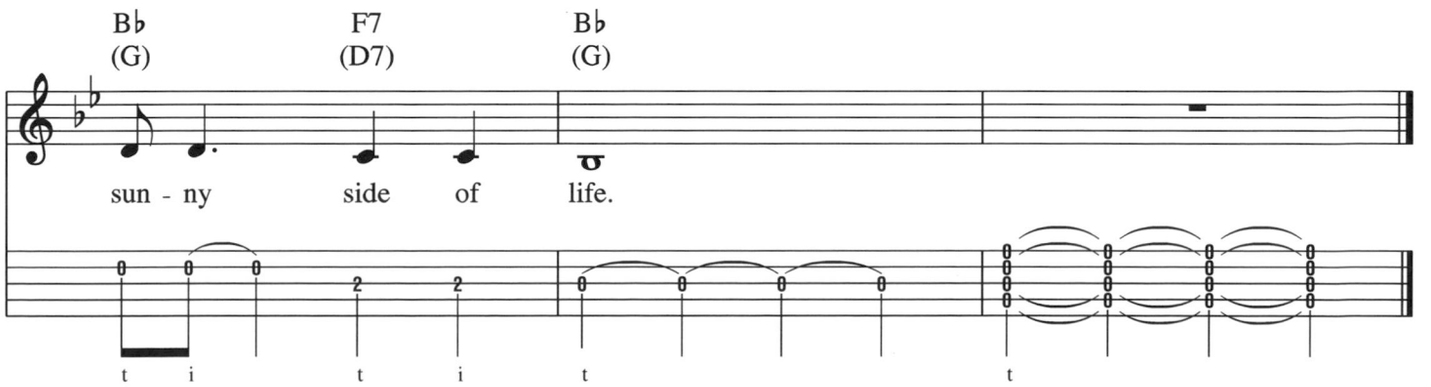

* Go back to the sign "𝄋" and play until ***"To Coda 1,"*** then skip ahead to the section labeled **"Coda 1."**
** Go back to the beginning.

I'll Fly Away

Words and Music by Albert E. Brumley

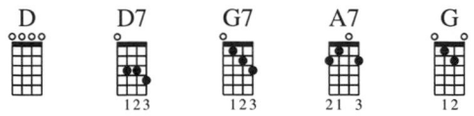

D tuning:
(5th-1st) F♯–D–F♯–A–D

Key of D

Moderately **Intro/Mandolin Solo**

D D7

G7 D

A7 D

To Coda 1

* Harm.

* Harmonics are produced by picking the note while the fret-hand lightly touches the string directly over the fret indicated.

© Copyright 1932 in "Wonderful Message" by Hartford Music Company
Renewed 1960 Albert E. Brumley & Sons (SESAC)/admin. by ICG
All Rights Reserved Used by Permission

Verse
D
D7
1. Some bright morn - in' when this life is o'er,
2. When the shad - ows of this life have gone,
3. Oh, how glad and hap - py when we meet.
4. Just a few more wea - ry days and then,
G
D
I'll fly a - way.
To that home on God's ce - les - tial shore.
Like a bird from these pris - on walls I'll fly.
No more cold iron shack - les on my feet.
To a land where joys will nev - er end,
A7
D
I'll fly a - way.

Chorus
D
D7
I'll fly a - way, oh glo - ry,
G
D
I'll fly a - way in the morn - in'.
When I die, hal - le - lu - jah by and by,
To Coda 2
1.
A7
D
I'll fly a - way.

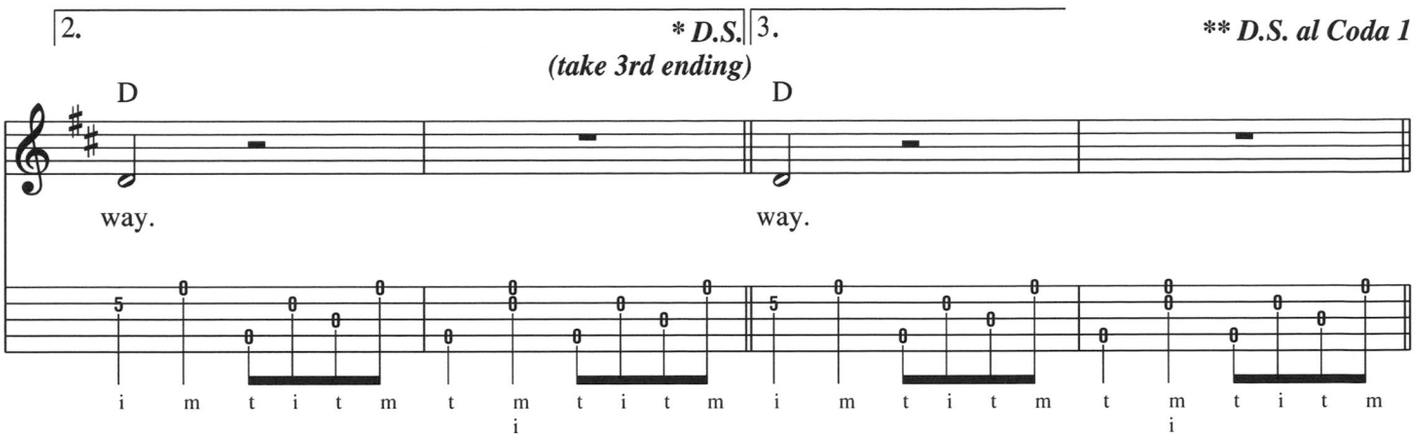

Coda 1

Chorus

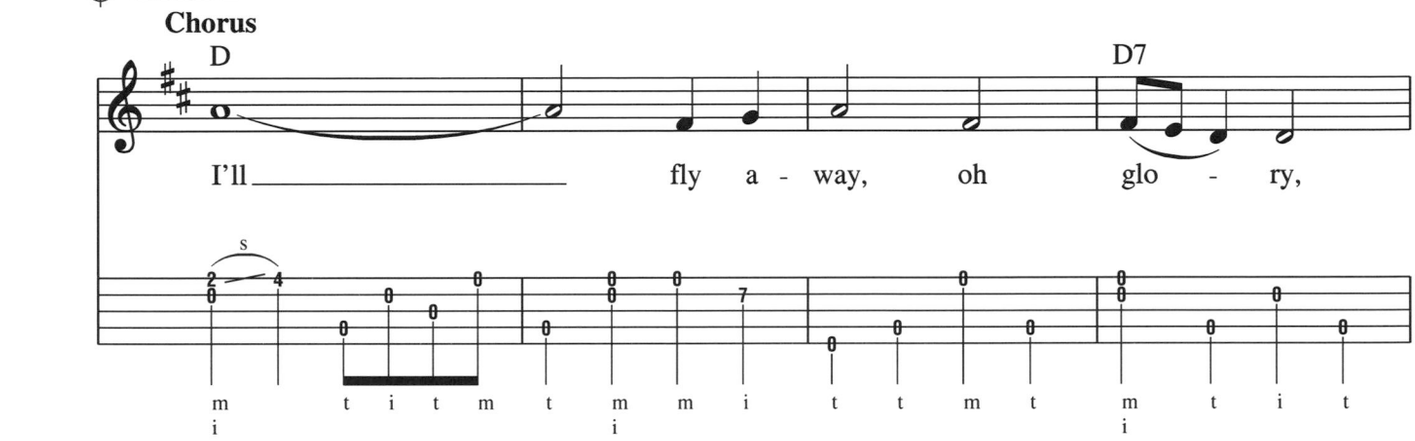

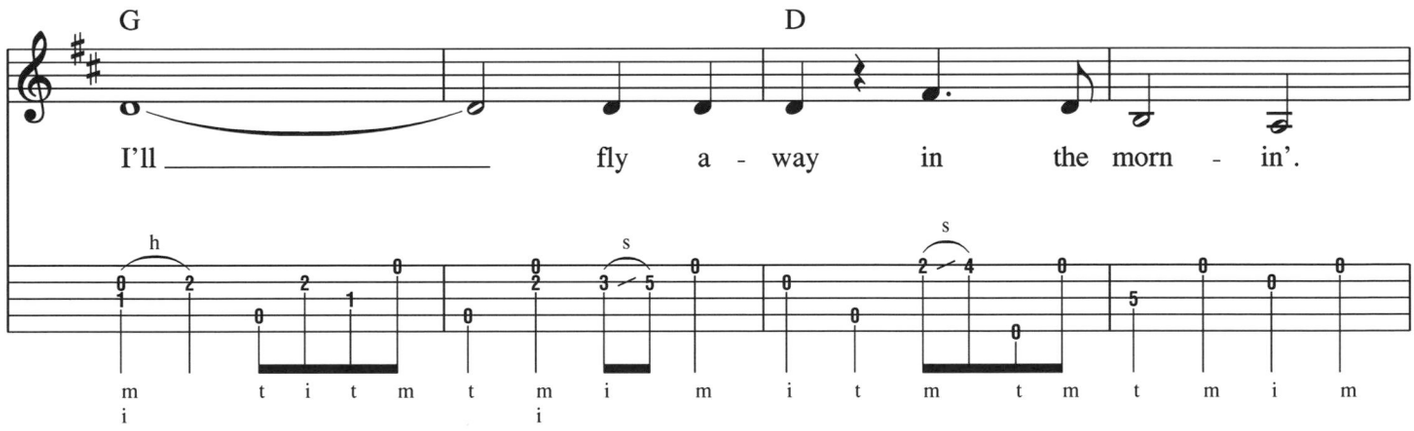

* Go back to the sign "𝄋"

** Go back to the sign "𝄋" and play until ***"To Coda 1,"*** then skip ahead to the section labeled "Coda 1."

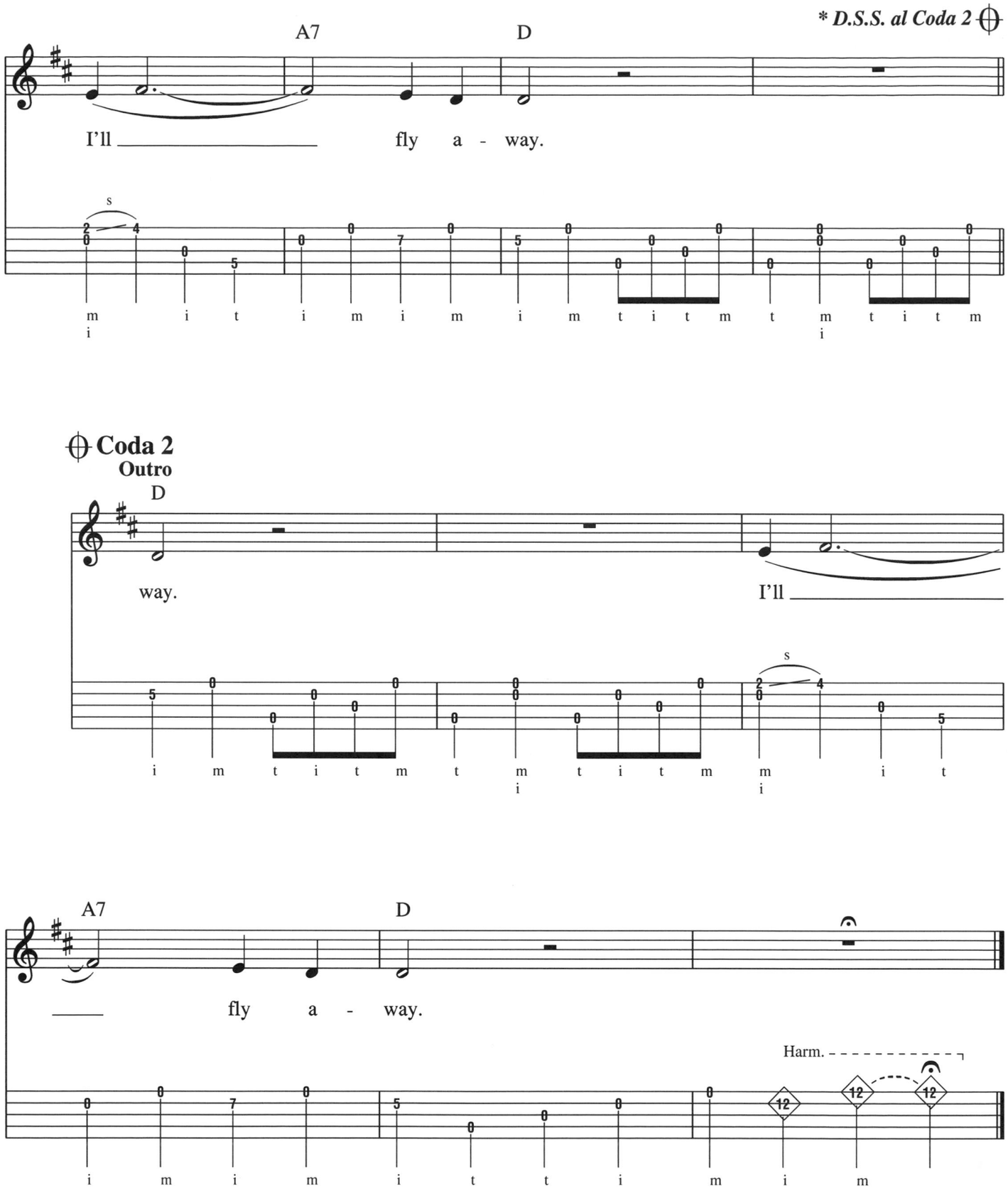

* Go back to the double sign "𝄋 𝄋" and play until ***"To Coda 2,"*** then skip ahead to the section labeled **"Coda 2."**

In the Highways

(I'll Be Somewhere Working for My Lord)

Words and Music by Maybelle Carter

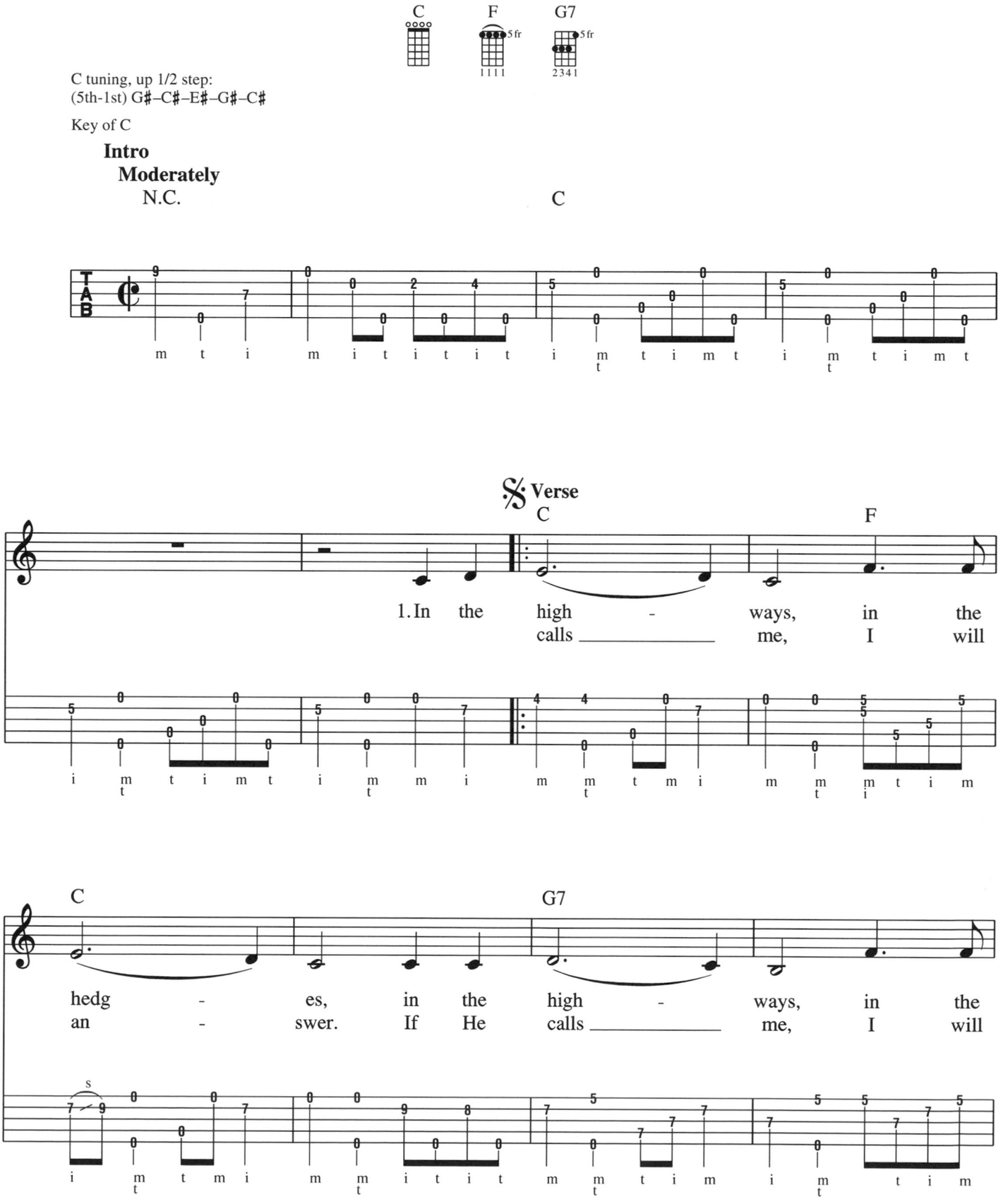

Copyright © 1965 by Peer International Corporation
Copyright Renewed
International Copyright Secured All Rights Reserved

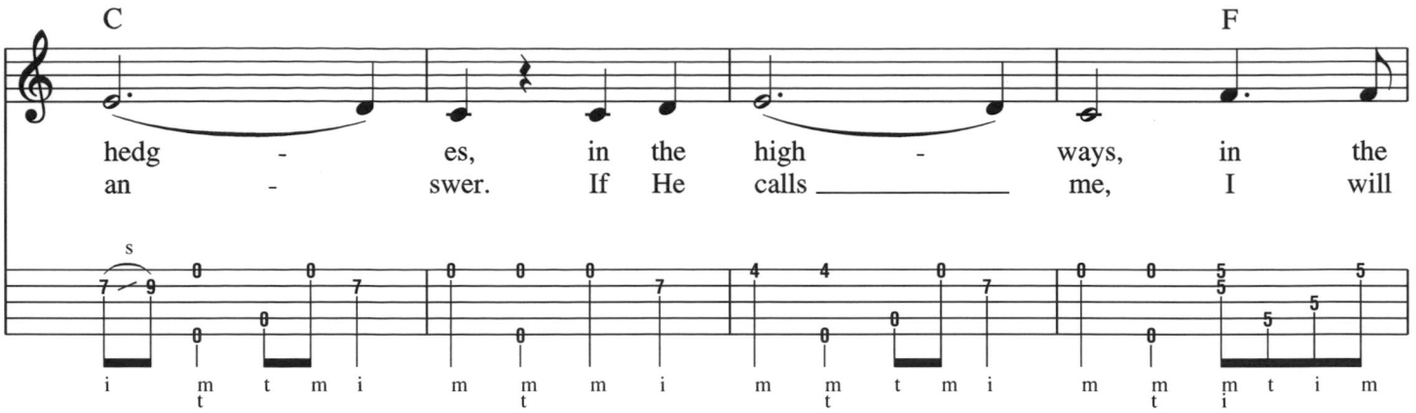
C
F
hedg - es, in the high - ways, in the
an - swer. If He calls me, I will

C
G7
To Coda
hedg - es,
an - swer.
I'll be some-where a work - ing for my

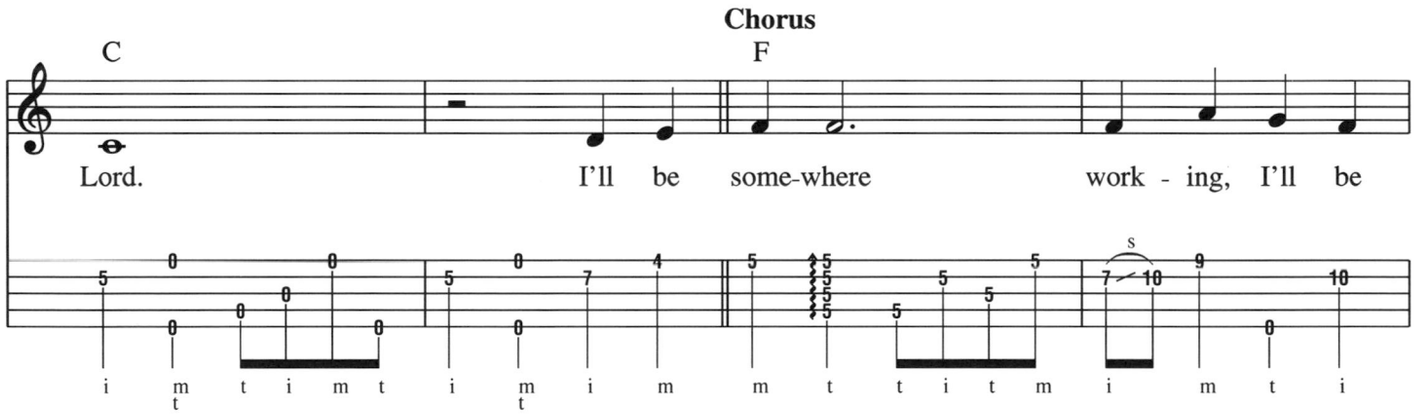
Chorus
C
F
Lord. I'll be some-where work - ing, I'll be

C
G7
some - where work - ing, I'll be some-where a work - ing for my

**** 2nd time, D.S. al Coda***
(take 1st lyrics)

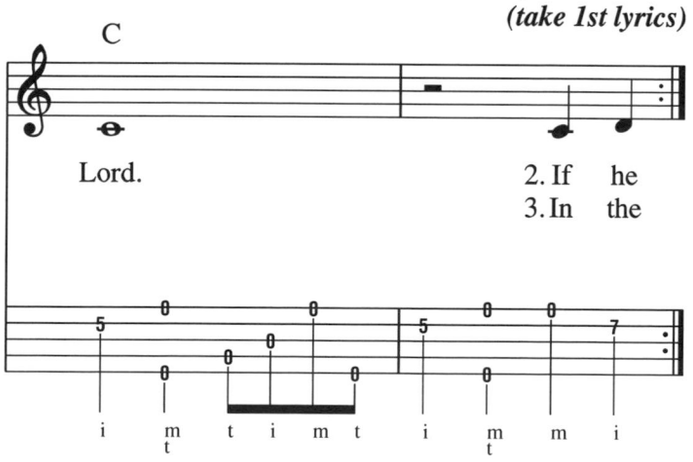

⊕ Coda

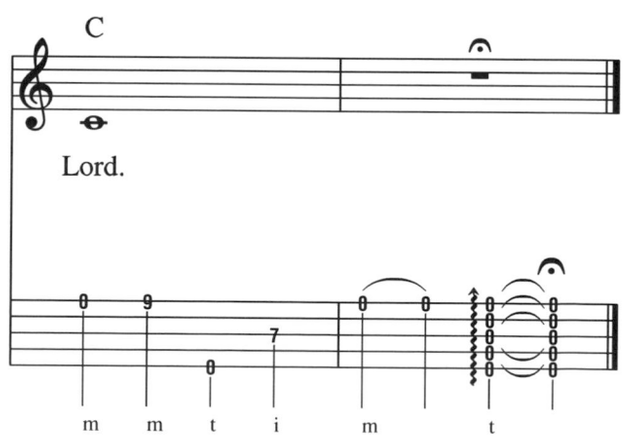

* Go back to the sign "𝄋" and play until ***"To Coda,"*** then skip ahead to the section labeled **"Coda."**

Didn't Leave Nobody but the Baby

Words and Music by Gillian Welch, T-Bone Burnett, Alan Lomax and Mrs. Sidney Carter

Tuning:
(5th-1st) B♭–D–G–B–D
Capo III

Key of B♭

Verse

Moderately in 2

N.C.

B♭

* (G)

1. Go to sleep, you lit - tle babe, go to sleep, you lit - tle babe. Your ma-ma's gone a - way and your dad-dy's gon - na stay, don't leave no - bod-y but the ba - by.

(Go to sleep you lit - tle babe, go to sleep you lit - tle babe.)

2.-6. *See additional lyrics*

1. - 5.

6.

2. Go to sleep, you lit-tle by.

* Symbol in parenthesis represents chord name respective to capoed banjo.
Symbol above reflects actual sounding chord. Capoed fret is "0" in tab.

Copyright © 2000 IRVING MUSIC, INC., SAY UNCLE MUSIC, HENRY BURNETT MUSIC
(BMI)/Administered by BUG MUSIC and GLOBAL JUKEBOX PUBLISHING (BMI)
All Rights for SAY UNCLE MUSIC Controlled and Administered by IRVING MUSIC, INC.
All Rights Reserved Used by Permission

2. Go to sleep, you little babe,
   (Go to sleep, you little babe.)
   Go to sleep, you little babe,
   (Go to sleep, you little babe.)
   Everybody's gone in the cotton and the corn,
   Didn't leave nobody but the baby.

3. You're sweet, little babe,
   (You're sweet, little babe.)
   You're sweet, little babe,
   (You're sweet, little babe.)
   Honey in the rock and the sugar don't stop.
   Gonna bring a bottle to the baby.

4. Don't you weep, pretty babe,
   (Don't you weep, pretty babe.)
   Don't you weep, pretty babe,
   (Don't you weep, pretty babe.)
   She's long gone with her red shoes on,
   Gonna need another lovin' baby.

5. Go to sleep, little babe,
   (Go to sleep, little babe.)
   Go to sleep, little babe,
   (Go to sleep, little babe.)
   You and me and the devil makes three,
   Don't need no other lovin' baby.

6. Go to sleep, you little babe,
   (Go to sleep, little babe.)
   Go to sleep, little babe,
   (Go to sleep, little babe.)
   Come lay your bones on the alabster stones
   And be my ever-lovin' baby.

I Am Weary (Let Me Rest)

Words and Music by Pete (Roberts) Kuykendall

Copyright © 1964 (Renewed 1997) Wynwood Music Co., Inc.
All Rights Reserved Used by Permission

D
round me. I am wear -
an - gels, fate has doomed
h
s

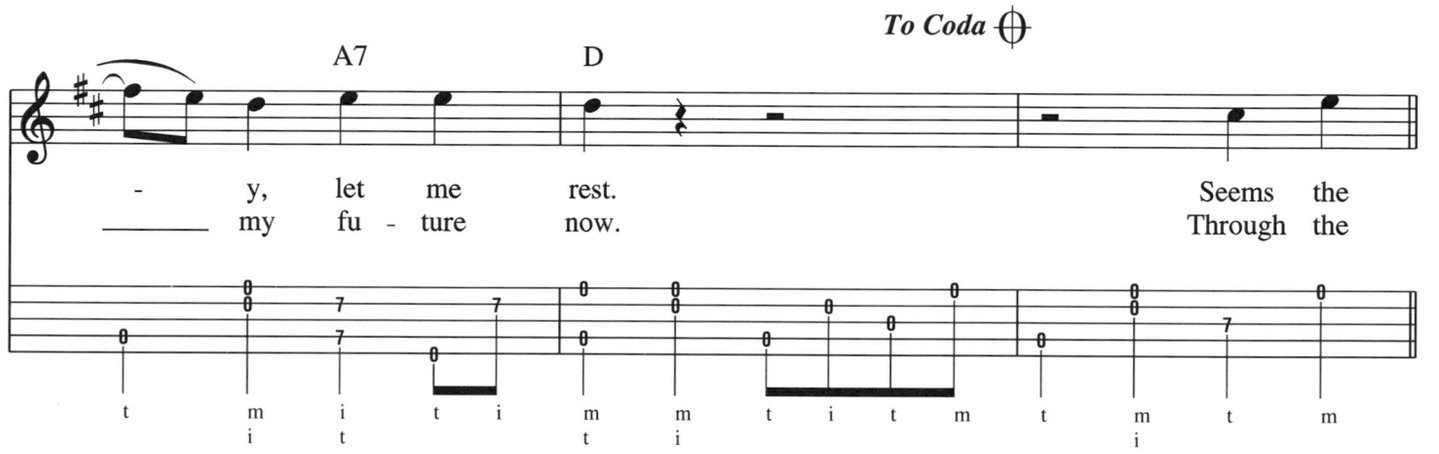
To Coda
A7
D
- y, let me rest. Seems the
my fu - ture now. Through the

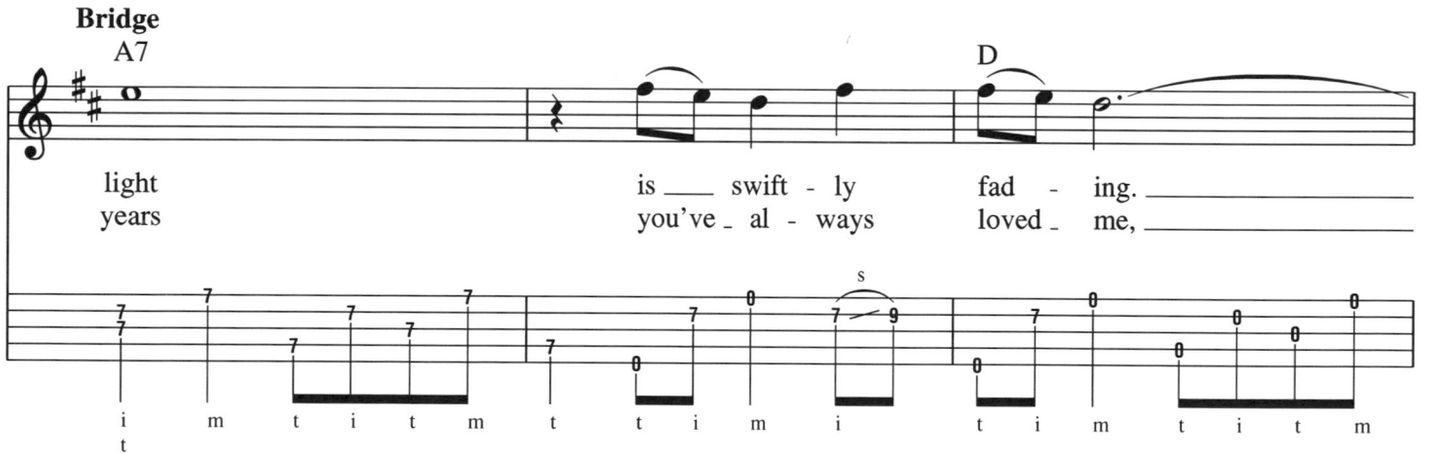
Bridge
A7
D
light is swift - ly fad - ing.
years you've al - ways loved me,
s

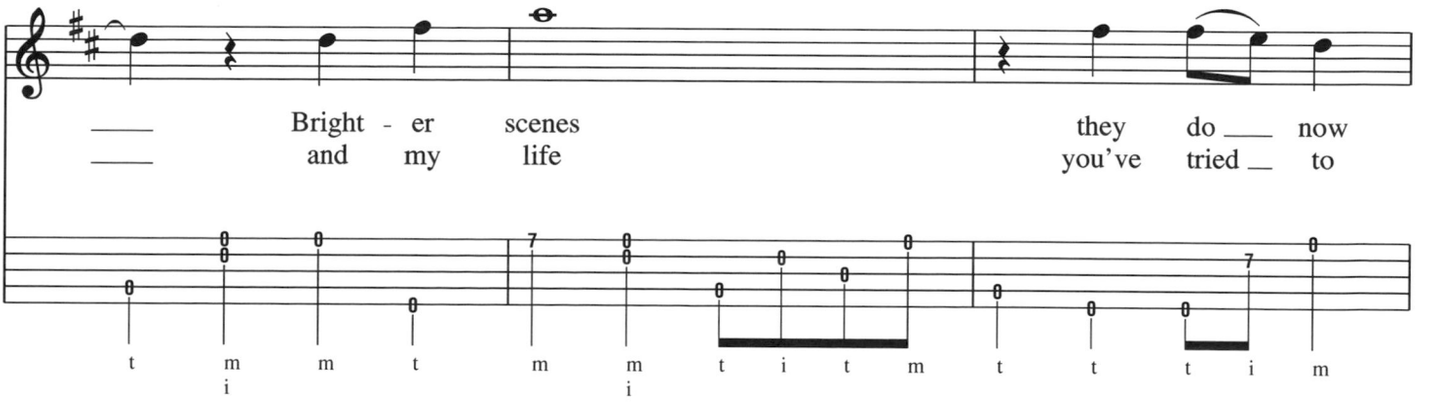
Bright - er scenes they do now
and my life you've tried to

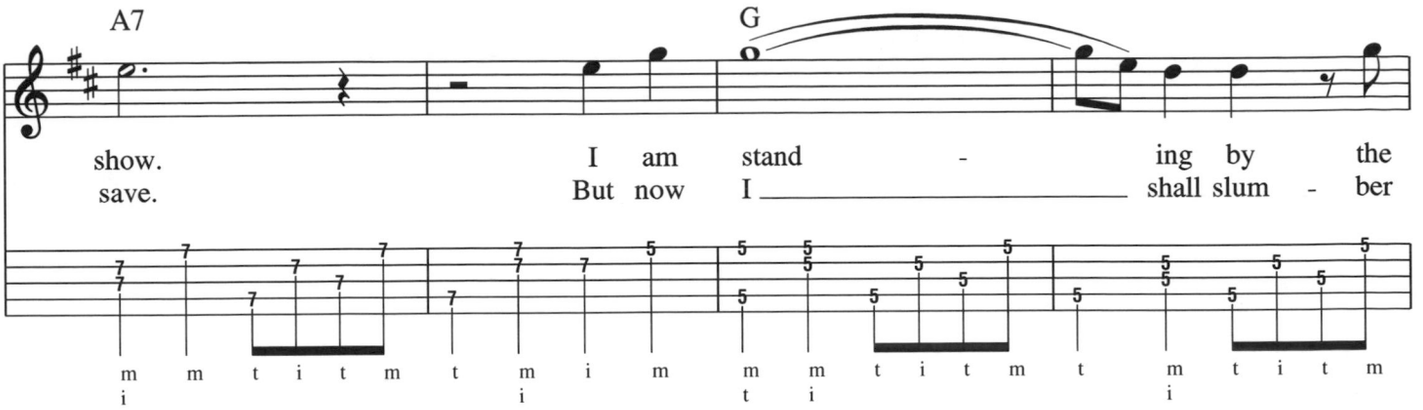

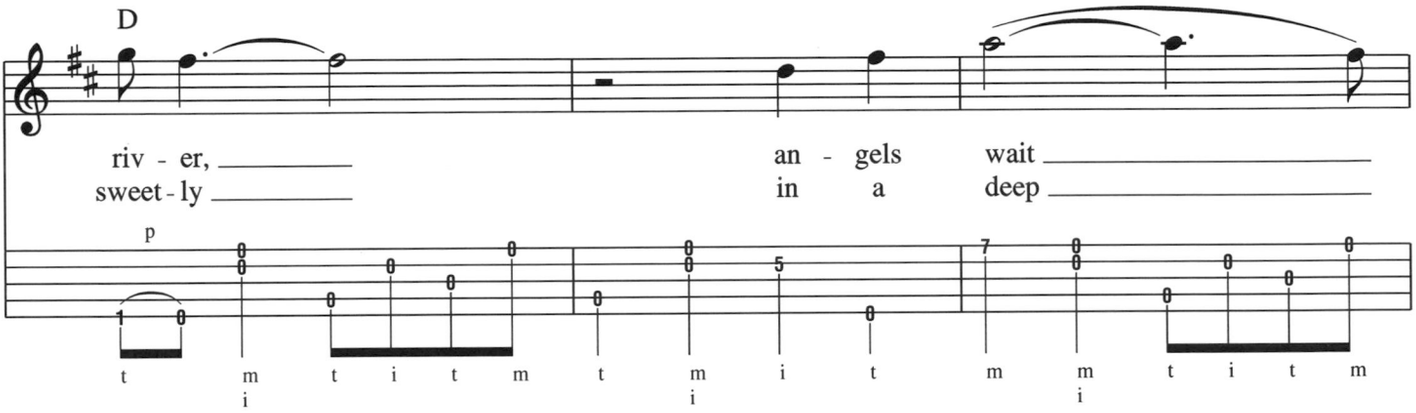

** 2nd time, D.S. al Coda*
(take 1st lyrics)

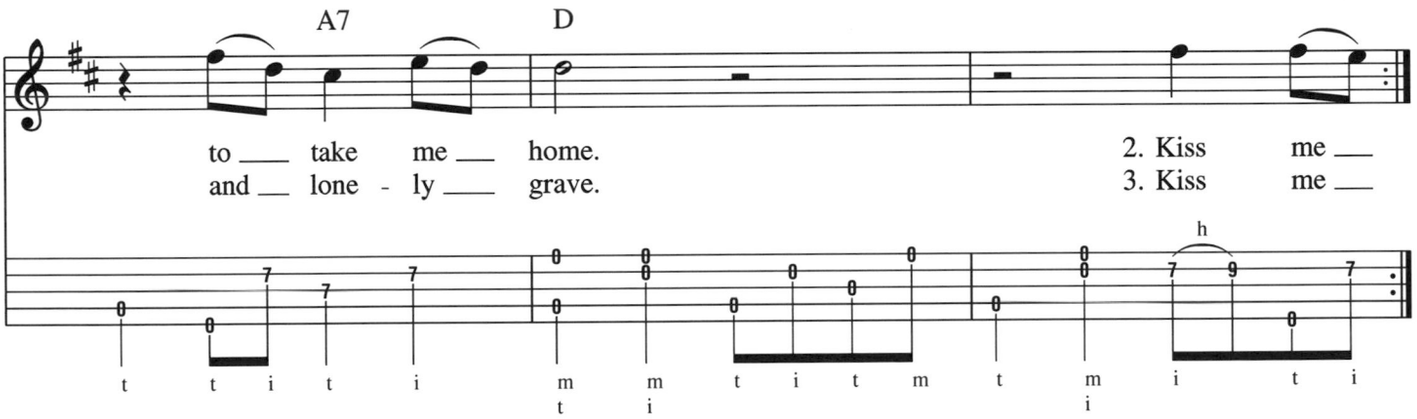

Coda

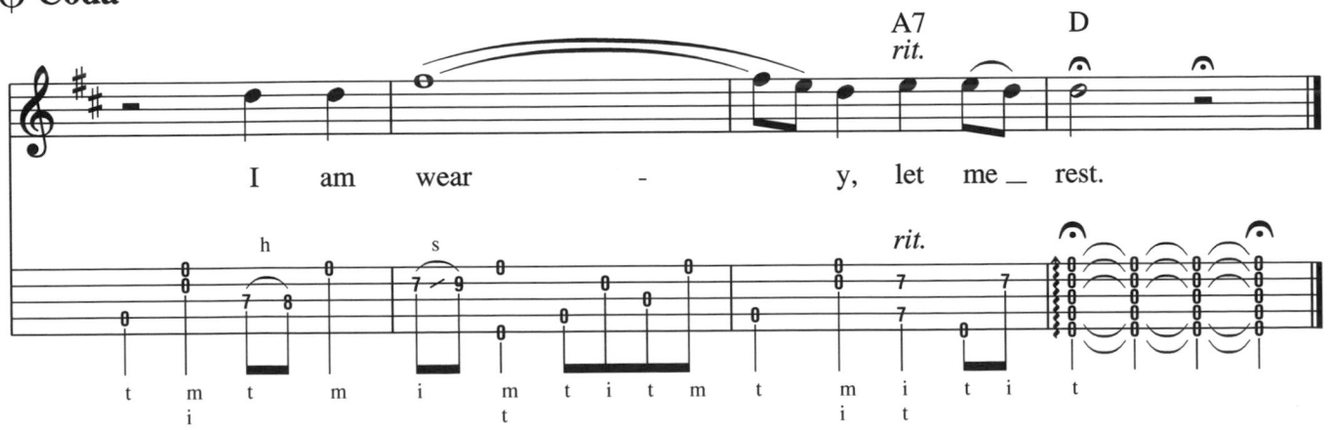

* Go back to the sign "𝄋" and play until *"To Coda,"* then skip ahead to the section labeled **"Coda."**

In the Jailhouse Now

Words and Music by Jimmie Rodgers

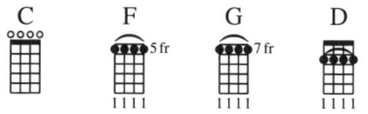

C tuning, down 1/2 step:
(5th-1st) F♯–B–F♯–B–D♯

Key of C

Intro
Moderately

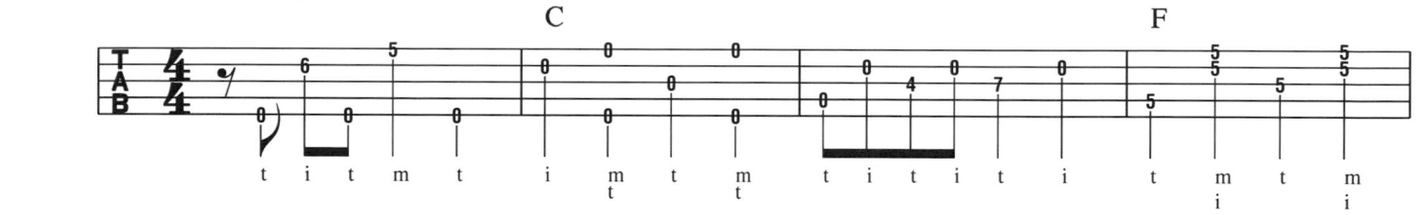

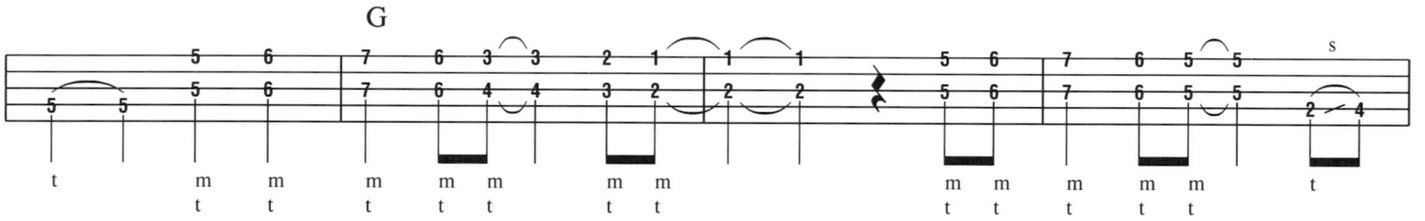

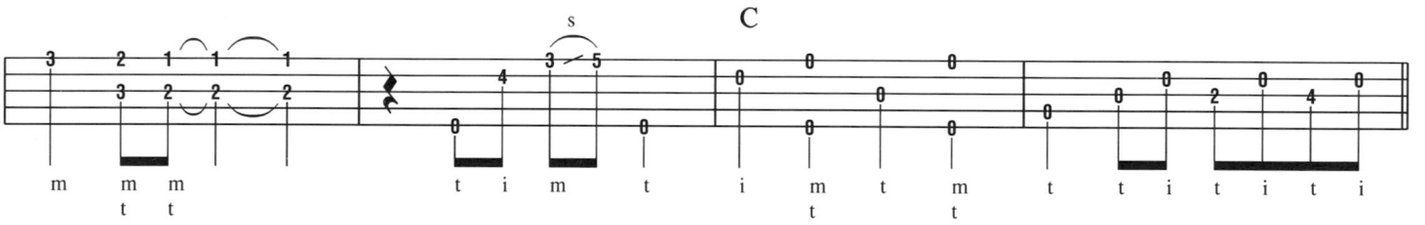

Verse

Copyright © 1928 by Peer International Corporation
Copyright Renewed
International Copyright Secured All Rights Reserved

gam - ble and rob. He thought he was the smart - est guy a -
eu - chre, but shoot - in' dice was his fav - 'rite
Su - sie. I said I was the swell - est guy a -
F
round. Well, I found out last
game. Well, he got throwed in
round. Well, we start - ed to spend - in' my
Mon - day that Bob got locked up Sun - day. They've
jail with no - bod - y to go his bail. The
mon - ey and she start - ed to call - in' me Hon - ey. We
D
G
got him in the jail - house way down - town.
judge done said that he re - fused the fine.
took in ev - 'ry cab - a - ret in town.

Chorus
N.C.
C
He's
He's
We're
in the jail - house now,
he's
he's
we're
in the jail - house
F
G
now.
Well, I
1., 2. told him once or twice
3. told that judge right
to stop play - in' cards and a shoot - in' dice.
to his face I don't like to see this place.
C
He's
We're
in the jail - house now.
Ah, dee, o, del,

Interlude
F
ay, hee, o, tee.
C
Ah, dee, o, del, ay, o, del, o, tee.
G
Yo, del, ay, hee, hee, yo, del, ay, hee, hee, yo, del,
C
1., 2.
3.
ay, hee.

I Am a Man of Constant Sorrow

Words and Music by Carter Stanley

Copyright © 1953 by Peer International Corporation
Copyright Renewed
International Copyright Secured All Rights Reserved

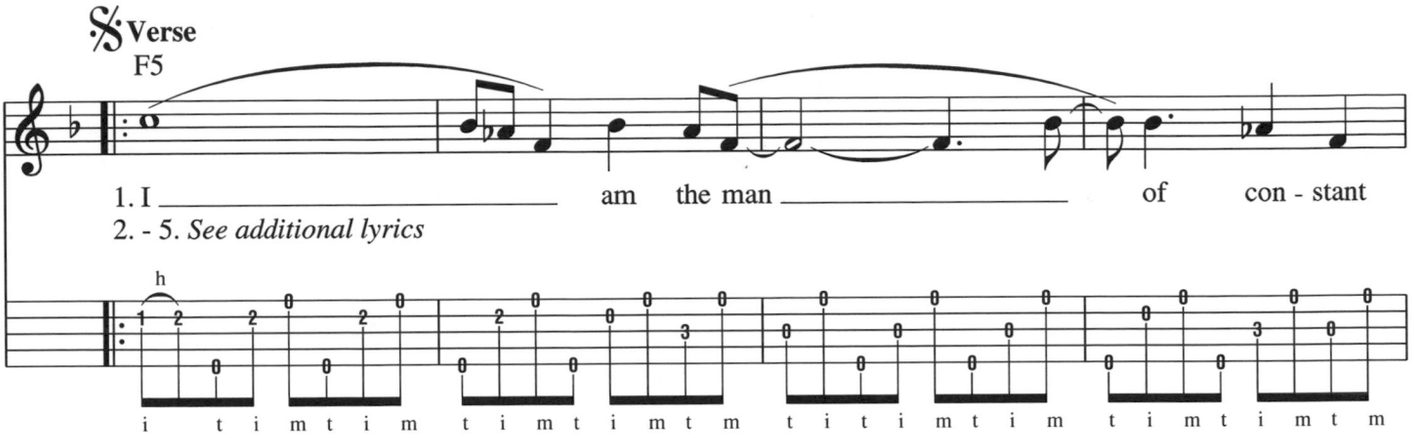
Verse
F5
1. I am the man of con - stant
2. - 5. See additional lyrics
h
i t i m t i m t i m t i m t m t i t i m t i m t i m t i m t m

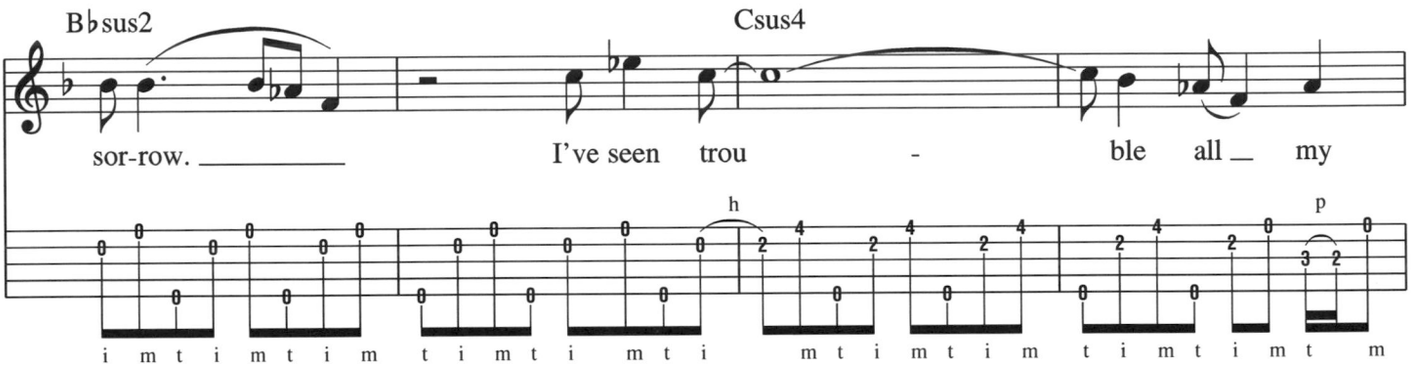
B♭sus2
Csus4
sor-row. I've seen trou - ble all my
h
p
i m t i m t i m t i m t i m t i m t i m t i m t i m t i m t m

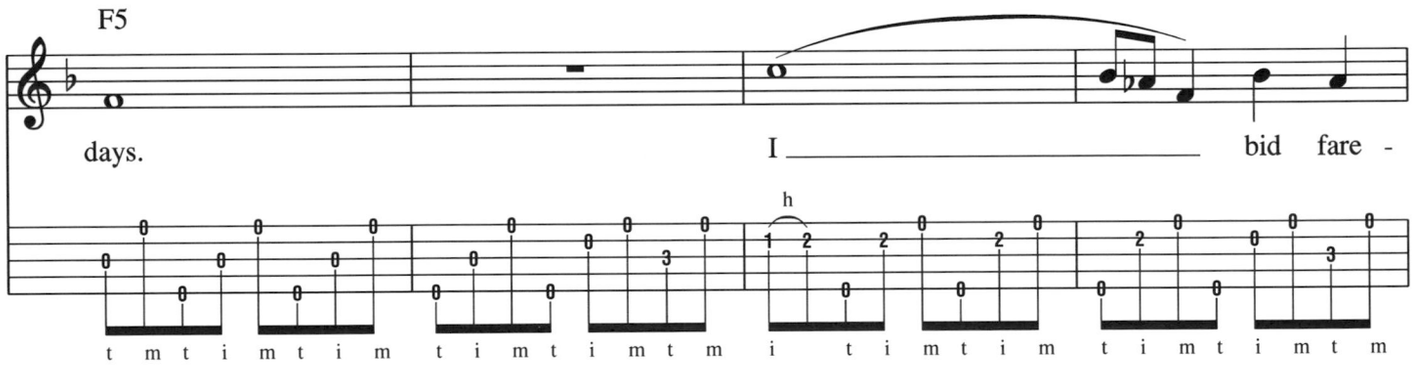
F5
days. I bid fare -
h
t m t i m t i m t i m t i m t m i t i m t i m t i m t i m t m

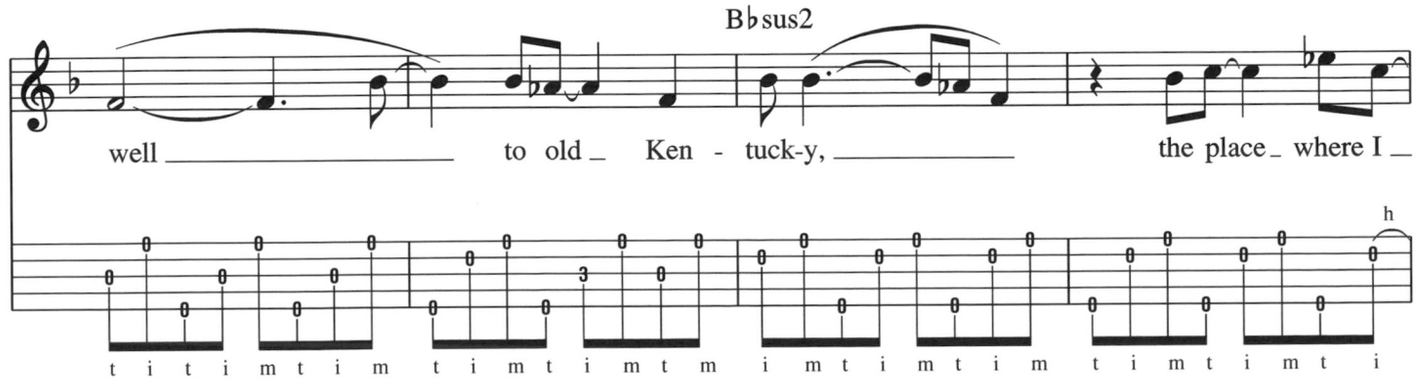
B♭sus2
well to old Ken - tuck-y, the place where I
h
t i t i m t i m t i m t i m t m i m t i m t i m t i m t i m t i

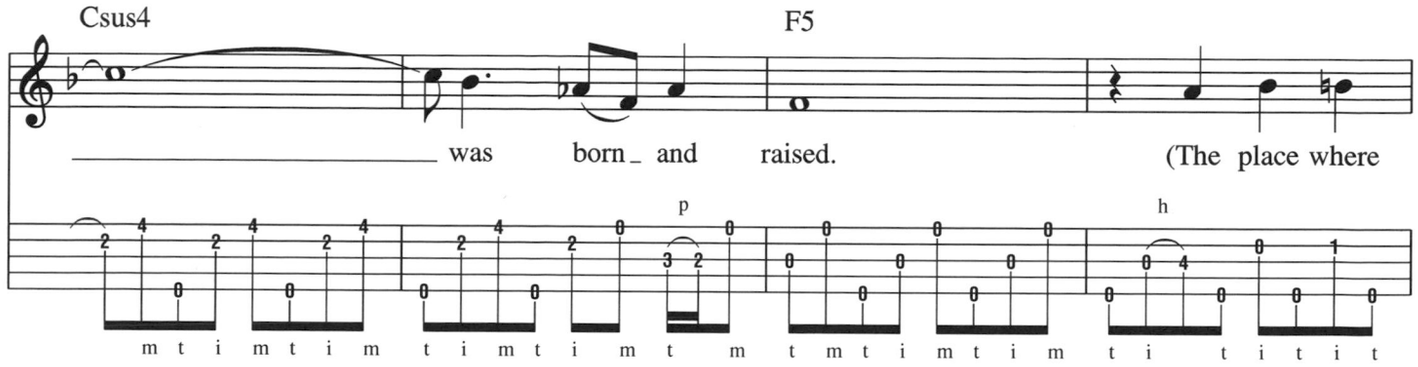
Csus4
F5
was born and raised.
(The place where

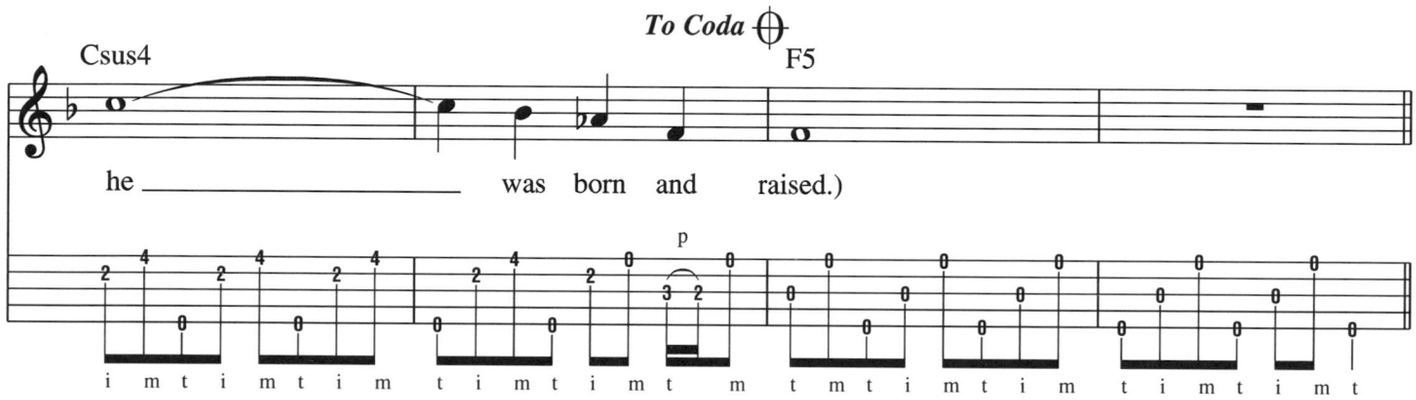
To Coda
Csus4
F5
he was born and raised.)

Banjo Solo

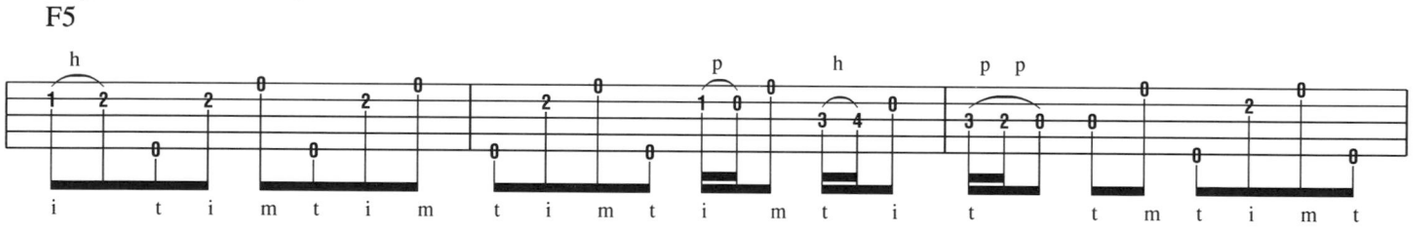
F5

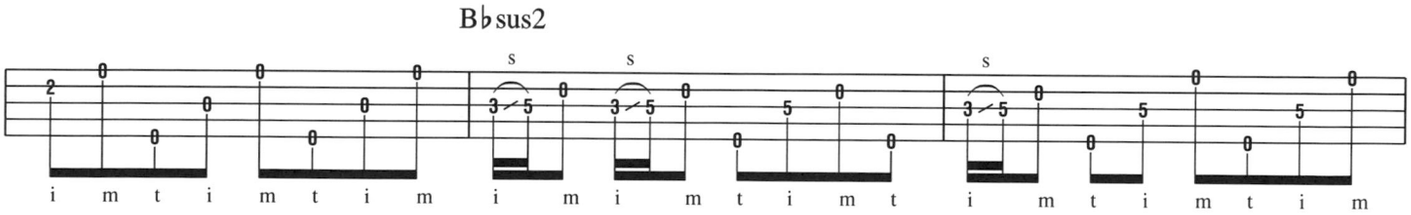
B♭sus2

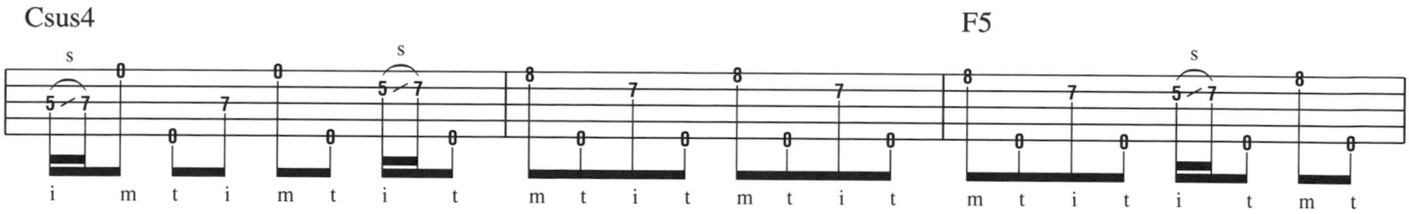
Csus4
F5

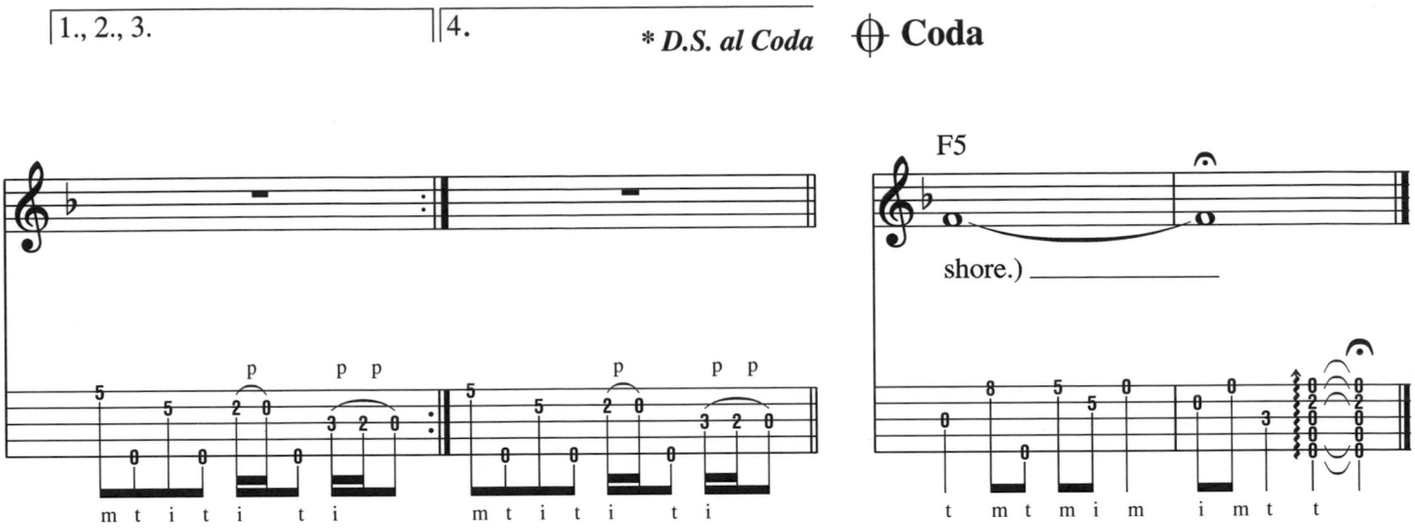

Additional Lyrics

2. For six long years I've been in trouble,
   No pleasure here on earth I've found.
   For in this world I'm bound to ramble.
   I have no friends to help me now.
   (He has no friends to help him now.)

3. It's fare thee well, my own true lover.
   I never expect to see you again.
   For I'm bound to ride that northern railroad.
   Perhaps I'll die upon that train.
   (Perhaps he'll die upon this train.)

4. You can bury me in sunny valley
   For many years where I may lay.
   Pray and you may learn to love another
   While I am sleeping in my grave.
   (While he is sleeping in his grave.)

5. Maybe your friends think I'm just a stranger,
   My face you never will see no more.
   But there is one promise that is given,
   I'll meet you on God's golden shore.
   (He'll meet you on God's golden shore.)

* Go back to the sign "𝄋" and play until ***"To Coda,"*** then skip ahead to the section labeled **"Coda."**

Angel Band

Words and Music by Ralph Stanley

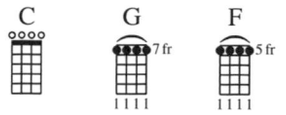

C tuning, down 1/2 step:
(5th-1st) F♯–B–F♯–B–D♯

Key of C

Intro
Moderately

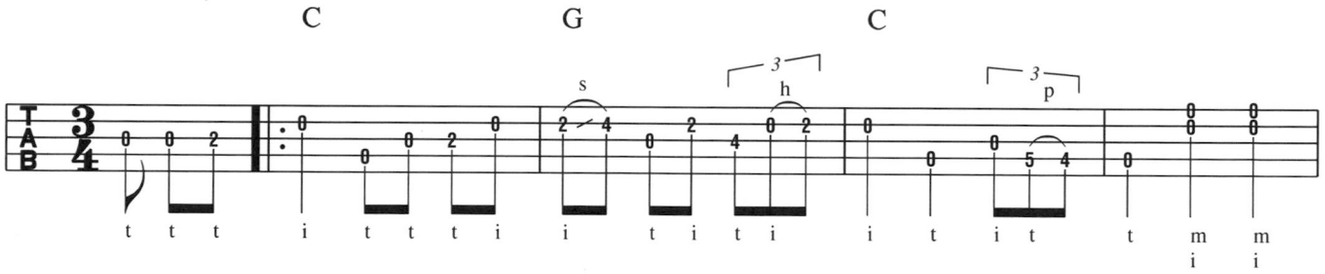

Verse

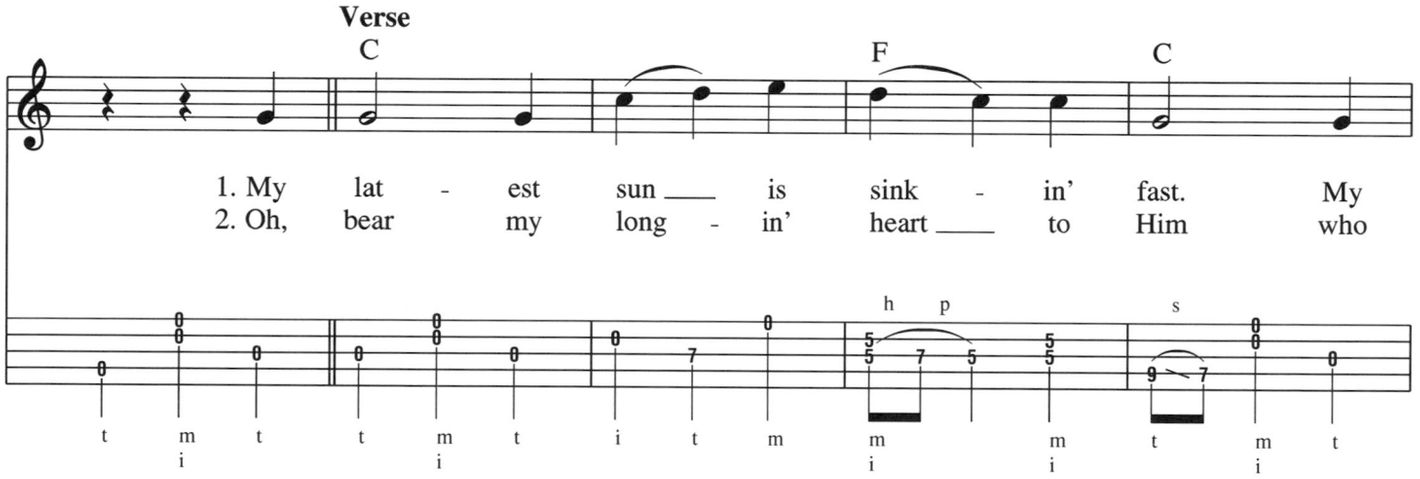

Copyright © 1958, 1978 by Fort Knox Music Inc. and Trio Music Company, Inc.
Copyright Renewed
International Copyright Secured All Rights Reserved
Used by Permission

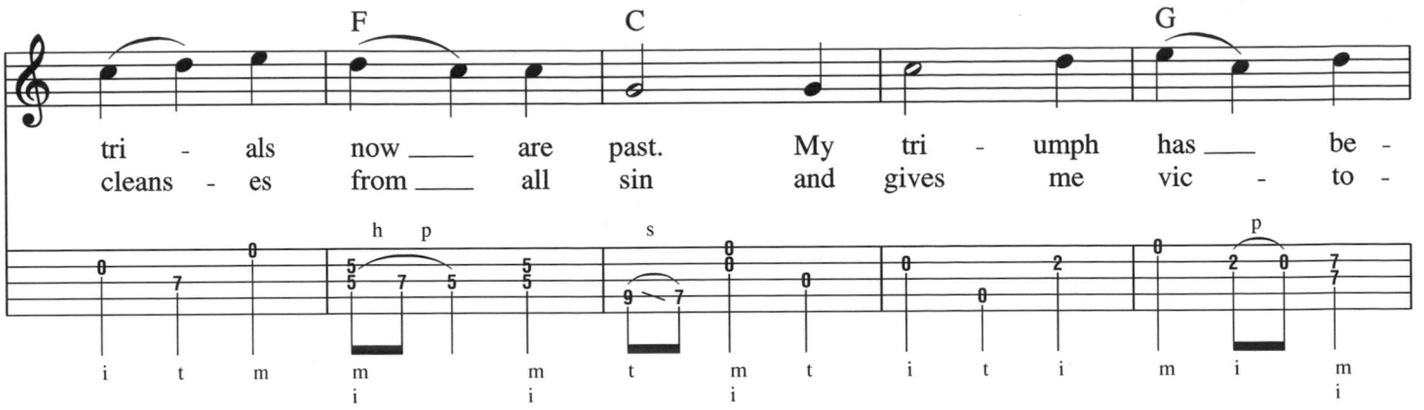
F C G
tri - als now ___ are past. My tri - umph has ___ be -
cleans - es from ___ all sin and gives me vic - to -
h p s p

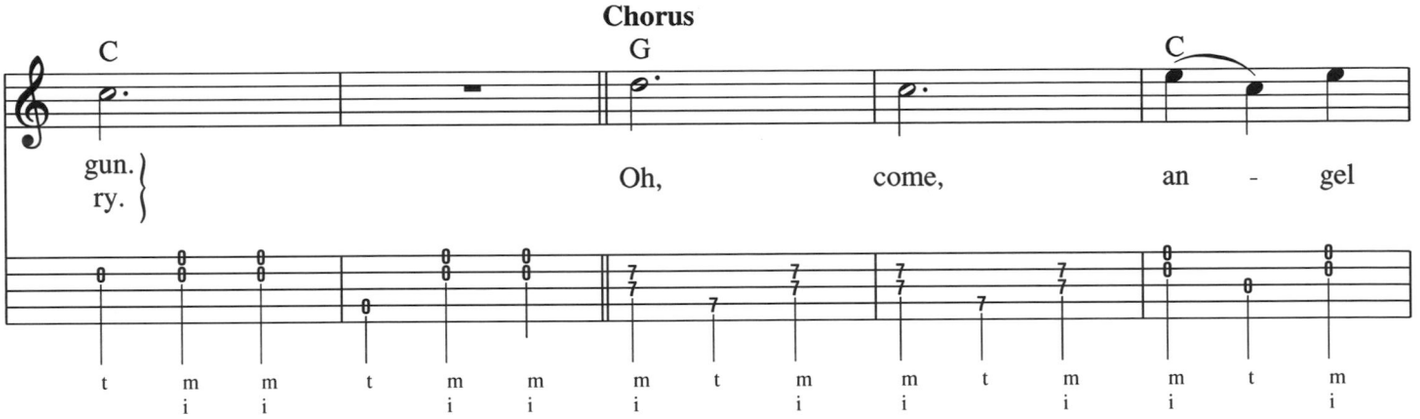
Chorus
C G C
gun.
ry.
Oh, come, an - gel

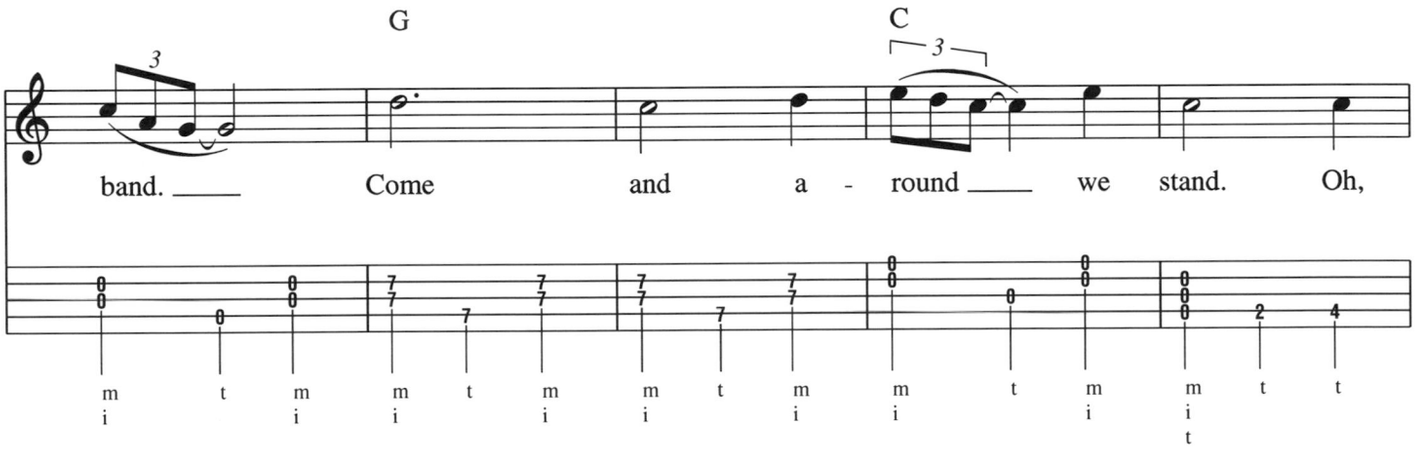
G C
3 3
band. ___ Come and a - round ___ we stand. Oh,

F C
3
bear me a - way on your snow __ white wings __ to my im -

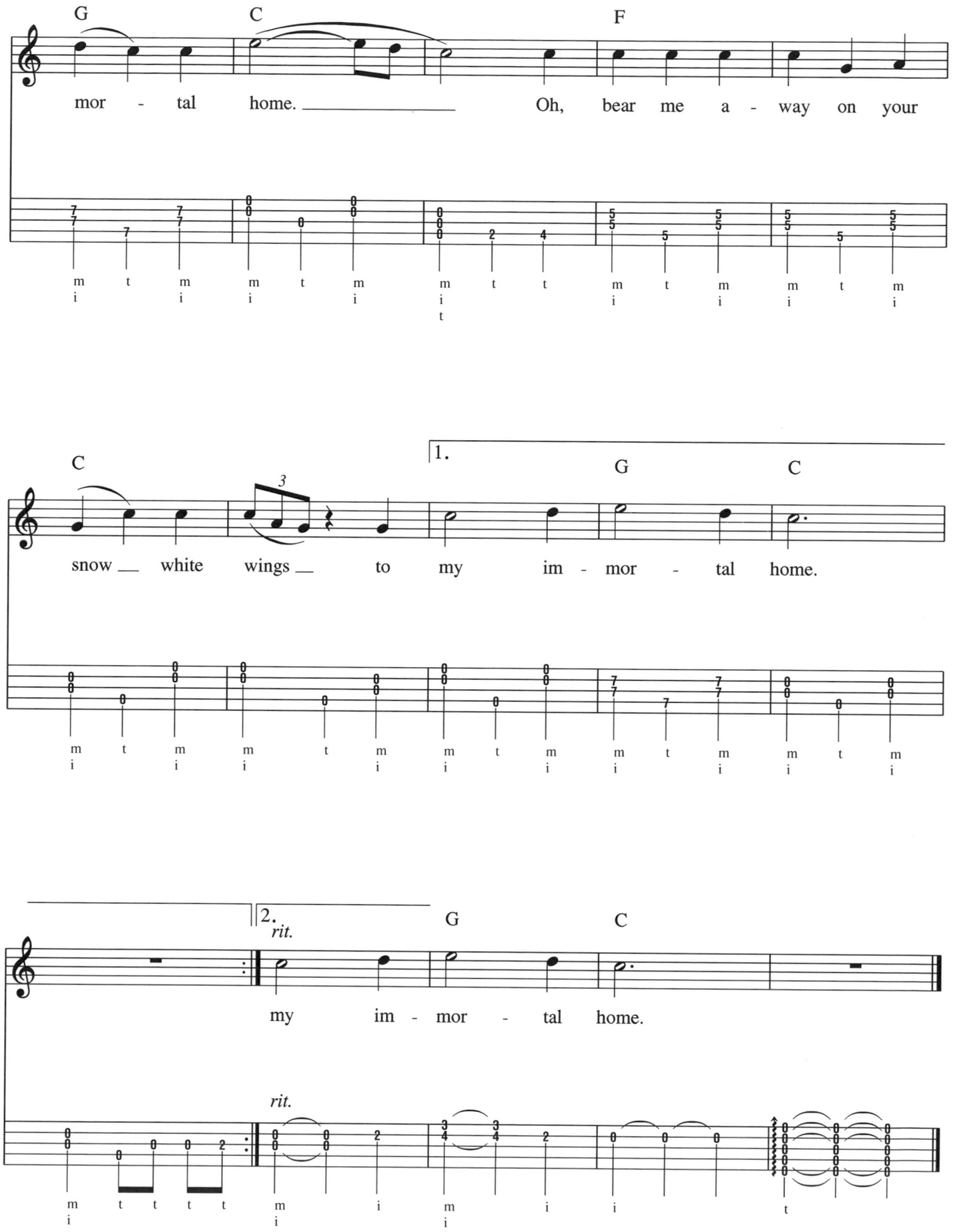
G C F
mor - tal home. Oh, bear me a - way on your
C 1. G C
snow white wings to my im - mor - tal home.
2. G C
rit.
my im - mor - tal home.
rit.

Banjo Notation Legend

TABLATURE graphically represents the banjo fingerboard. Each horizontal line represents a string, and each number represents a fret.

Strings: 1 D, 2 B, 3 G, 4 D, 5 G

4th string, 2nd fret — 1st & 2nd strings open, played together

TIME SIGNATURE:
The upper number indicates the number of beats per measure, the lower number indicates that a quarter note gets one beat.

CUT TIME:
Each note's time value should be cut in half. As a result, the music will be played twice as fast as it is written.

QUARTER NOTE:
time value = 1 beat

EIGHTH NOTES:
time value = 1/2 beat each

single — in series

SIXTEENTH NOTES:
time value = 1/4 beat each

single — in series

DOTTED QUARTER NOTE:
time value = 1 1/2 beat

TIE: Pick the 1st note only, then let it sustain for the combined time value.

TRIPLET: Three notes played in the same time normally occupied by two notes of the same time value.

GRACE NOTE: A quickly played note with no time value of its own. The grace note and the note following it only occupy the time value of the second note.

RITARD: A gradual slowing of the tempo or speed of the song.

rit.

QUARTER REST:
time value = 1 beat of silence

EIGHTH REST:
time value = 1/2 beat of silence

HALF REST:
time value = 2 beats of silence

WHOLE REST:
time value = 4 beats of silence

ENDINGS: When a repeated section has a first and second ending, play the first ending only the first time and play the second ending only the second time.

1. 2.

REPEAT SIGNS: Play the music between the repeat signs two times.

D.S. AL CODA:
Play through the music until you complete the measure labeled *"D.S. al Coda,"* then go back to the sign (𝄋). Then play until you complete the measure labeled *"To Coda ⊕,"* then skip to the section labeled "⊕ Coda."

𝄋 — *To Coda* ⊕ — *D.S. al Coda* — ⊕ *Coda*

HAMMER-ON: Strike the first (lower) note with one finger, then sound the higher note (on the same string) with another finger by fretting it without picking.

h

PULL-OFF: Place both fingers on the notes to be sounded. Strike the first note and without picking, pull the finger off to sound the second (lower) note.

p

SLIDE UP: Strike the first note and then slide the same fret-hand finger up to the second note. The second note is not struck.

s

SLIDE DOWN: Strike the first note and then slide the same fret-hand finger down to the second note. The second note is not struck.

s

HALF-STEP CHOKE: Strike the note and bend the string up 1/2 step.

1/2

WHOLE-STEP CHOKE: Strike the note and bend the string up one step.

1

NATURAL HARMONIC: Strike the note while the fret-hand lightly touches the string directly over the fret indicated.

Harm.

BRUSH: Play the notes of the chord indicated by quickly rolling them from bottom to top.

Scruggs/Keith Tuners:

HALF-TWIST UP: Strike the note, twist tuner up 1/2 step, and continue playing.

1/2

HALF-TWIST DOWN: Strike the note, twist tuner down 1/2 step, and continue playing.

1/2

WHOLE-TWIST UP: Strike the note, twist tuner up one step, and continue playing.

1

1

Right Hand Fingerings

t = thumb i = index finger m = middle finger